Show me

PCs

A Visual Guide to the Basics

Joe Kraynak

See how easy
using a PC can be

Colorful illustra-
tions show you
each step

a

alpha
books

A Division of Prentice Hall Computer Publishing
1711 North College Avenue, Carmel, Indiana 46032 USA

International Standard Book Number: 1-56761-260-1
Library of Congress Catalog Card Number: 93-71511

95 94 93   8 7 6 5 4 3 2 1

Interpretation of the printing code: the rightmost number of the first series of numbers is the year of the book's printing; the rightmost number of the second series of numbers is the number of the book's printing. For example, a printing code of 93-1 shows that the first printing of the book occurred in 1993.

Screen reproductions in this book were created by means of the program Collage Plus from Inner Media, Inc., Hollis, NH.

Printed in the United States of America

TRADEMARKS

Publisher   *Marie Butler-Knight*
Associate Publisher   *Lisa A. Bucki*
Managing Editor   *Elizabeth Keaffaber*
Acquisitions Manager   *Stephen R. Poland*
Development Editor   *Seta Frantz*
Manuscript Editor   *San Dee Phillips*
Cover Designer   *Scott Fulmer*
Designer   *Roger Morgan*
Indexer   *Jeanne Clark*
Production Team   *Diana Bigham, Scott Cook, Tim Cox, Howard Jones, Tom Loveman, Beth Rago, Greg Simsic*

Special thanks to C. Herbert Feltner for ensuring the technical accuracy of this book.

CONTENTS

Part 5 Making Your Computer Do Something Useful 87

Glossary 107

Index 115

INTRODUCTION

Have you ever said to yourself, "I wish someone would just *show me* how to use a personal computer?" If you have, this Show Me book is for you. In it, you won't find detailed explanations of what's going on inside your computer each time you enter a command. Instead, you will see pictures that *show you* what a computer is, what it can do for you, and how to use it.

This book will make you feel as though you have your very own personal trainer standing next to you, pointing at the screen and keyboard, and showing you exactly what to do.

HOW TO USE THIS BOOK

Using this book is as simple as falling off your chair. Just flip to the topic or task that you want to learn and follow the pictures. You will see easy step-by-step instructions that tell you which keys to press and which commands to select. You will also see step-by-step pictures that show you what to do. Follow the steps or the pictures (or both) to complete the task.

Changing Disk Drives

1. Make sure there is a disk in the drive you want to change to. (If the disk is blank, it must be formatted. If the disk has files on it, it is already formatted.)

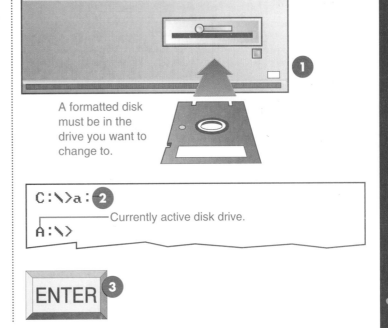

A formatted disk must be in the drive you want to change to.

2. Type the letter of the drive followed by a colon.

```
C:\>a: 2
```
Currently active disk drive.
```
A:\>
```

3. Press Enter.

ENTER 3

Definitions in Plain English

In addition to the basic step-by-step approach, pages may contain Learn the Lingo definitions to help you understand key terms. These definitions are placed off to the side, so you can easily skip them.

1

Tips and Shortcuts

Throughout this book, you will encounter tips that provide important information about a task or shortcuts that tell you how to perform the task more quickly.

TIP

Keyboard Shortcuts Here are some keyboard shortcuts for opening and saving files and for exiting a Windows program:

Open File	Ctrl+O
Save File	Ctrl+S
Exit	Ctrl+X

Exercises

Because most people learn by doing, I have added some exercises throughout the book to give you additional practice performing a task.

Exercise

Take the following steps to make a directory at the DOS prompt, change to the directory, and delete it:

1 Type **cd** and press **Enter** to change to the root directory.

2 Type **md testdir** and press **Enter** to make the TESTDIR directory.

3 Type **cd\testdir** and press **Enter** to change to the TESTDIR directory.

4 Type **cd** and press **Enter** to change back to the root directory.

5 Type **rd testdir** and press **Enter** to remove the TESTDIR directory.

```
C:\DATA\JOE>cd\

C:\>md testdir

C:\>cd\testdir

C:\TESTDIR>cd\

C:\>rd testdir

C:\>
```

2

Buttons to Push and Keys to Press

Every computer book has its own way of telling you which buttons to push and which keys to press. Here's how I have handled those formalities:

- Keys that you should press appear as they do on your keyboard; for example, press Alt or press F10. If you need to press more than one key at once, the keys are separated with plus signs. For example, if the text tells you to press Alt+F, hold down the Alt key while pressing the F key.

- Text that you should type is printed in **boldface type like this**.

- Some commands are activated by selecting a menu and then an option. If I tell you to "select **F**ile **N**ew," you should open the **F**ile menu and select the **N**ew option. In this book, the selection letter is printed in boldface for easy recognition.

Where Should You Start?

If this is your first encounter with computers, look at Part 1, "Quick Computer Tour," before moving on to the other parts. You will learn about the parts of the computer, how to start it, and what goes on inside your computer as you work.

Once you know the basics, you can work through this book from beginning to end or skip around from task to task, as needed. If you decide to skip around, there are several ways you can find what you're looking for:

- Use the Table of Contents at the front of this book to find a specific task or topic you want to learn about.

- Use the complete index at the back of this book to look up a specific task or topic and find the page number on which it is covered.

- Use the color-coded sections to find groups of related tasks and topics.

- Flip through the book, and look at the task and topic titles at the top of the pages. This method works best if you know the general location of the task in the book.

PART 1

Quick Computer Tour

If you don't know a system unit from a shoe box or a monitor from a TV screen, this part will teach you the least you need to know to get started.

- The Parts of a Computer

- Understanding the System Unit

- What Goes on Inside Your Computer?

- How a Computer Functions

- Understanding Memory

- The Central Processing Unit

THE PARTS OF A COMPUTER

What Is a Computer?

A computer is not a single, unified machine. It consists of a system unit that provides the thinking power and data storage for the computer and several other parts that allow you to get data and information into and out of the system unit.

There are two types of software: operating system software and applications. Operating system software provides the fundamental instructions that tell the system unit how to save and process data; how to communicate with the printer, keyboard, and other devices; and how to run other programs (applications). The most common operating system is MS-DOS, which stands for Microsoft Disk Operating System. Applications are programs that allow you to perform a specific task such as write a letter, balance a checkbook, or draw a picture. When you run an application, the operating system fades into the background.

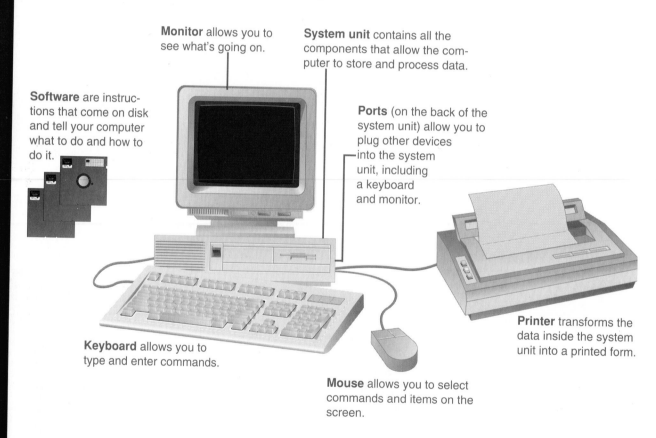

Monitor allows you to see what's going on.

System unit contains all the components that allow the computer to store and process data.

Software are instructions that come on disk and tell your computer what to do and how to do it.

Ports (on the back of the system unit) allow you to plug other devices into the system unit, including a keyboard and monitor.

Keyboard allows you to type and enter commands.

Mouse allows you to select commands and items on the screen.

Printer transforms the data inside the system unit into a printed form.

UNDERSTANDING THE SYSTEM UNIT

What's Inside the System Unit?

The system unit is like your head; it contains all the components that allow your system to store and process data and communicate with other parts of the computer.

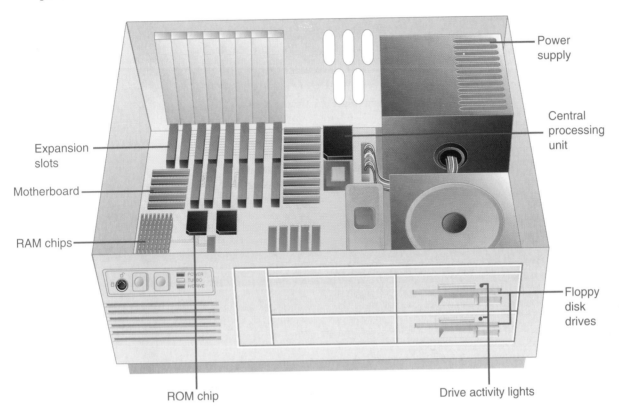

Power supply

Central processing unit

Expansion slots

Motherboard

RAM chips

ROM chip

Floppy disk drives

Drive activity lights

LEARNING THE LINGO

RAM: Rhymes with "mam" and stands for random-access memory. Whenever you run a program or type data, the program and data are stored in RAM (frequently called *memory*). Because RAM depends on electricity in order to function, if you turn off your computer, RAM forgets everything.

ROM: Rhymes with "mom" and stands for read-only memory. This is a special type of memory that the manufacturer uses to store your computer's permanent startup instructions. Typically, you cannot change the instructions that are stored in ROM.

Floppy disk: A wafer encased in plastic that magnetically stores data (the facts and figures you enter and save).

Hard disk: A disk that is permanently sealed inside a hard disk drive. Hard disks store more data than do floppy disks.

What It Is	What It Does
On/Off switch	Turns the power to the computer on or off.
Power supply	Regulates the flow of current to the motherboard and disk drives.
Motherboard	Contains the "thinking" parts of the computer, including the memory and processing chips.
Central processing unit (CPU)	Processes all of the data that flows through the system unit.
RAM (random-access memory)	Stores data and program instructions for the CPU.
ROM (read-only memory)	Stores the basic instructions your computer needs to start and function.
Expansion slots	Allows you to connect additional circuit boards to the motherboard.
Floppy disk drives	Allow the system unit to read data off floppy disks and write data onto disks.
Hard disk drive	(Usually inside the system unit) acts like a giant floppy disk drive complete with nonremovable disks.
Reset button	Clears the computer's memory if the computer ever refuses to respond to your commands.
Turbo button	(On some system units) allows you to set your computer to maximum speed or slower.
Drive activity lights	Show when a disk drive is reading data off a disk or writing data to a disk.
Keyboard lock	(On some system units) allows you to lock the keyboard so nobody else can use your computer without your permission.

WHAT GOES ON INSIDE YOUR COMPUTER?

What Happens Inside?

Here is a general description of what happens inside your computer when you start it, run an application, or perform other tasks:

Power-On Self Test (POST)   When you turn on your computer, electricity flows through the power supply to the ROM-BIOS chip, which contains the permanent startup instructions for the computer. The ROM-BIOS instructs the CPU to check the parts of the computer, to make sure everything is connected and working properly. This check is called the Power-On Self Test (POST).

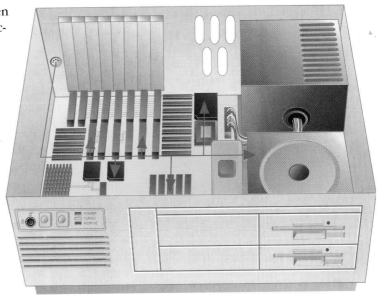

Test Results   The CPU compares the information it gathered to information stored in your computer's CMOS. CMOS stores information about all the components that your computer contains. If the information matches, the BIOS gives your computer the OK to load DOS.

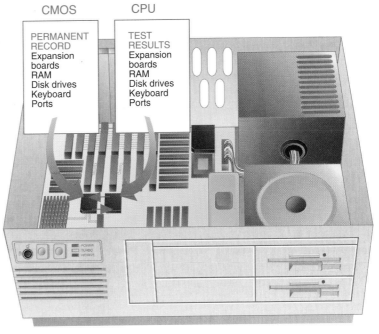

WHAT GOES ON INSIDE YOUR COMPUTER?

Loading the Operating System

After the Power-On Self Test, your computer reads the operating system instructions (DOS) from disk into its memory. The operating system works behind the scenes to manage the computer operations.

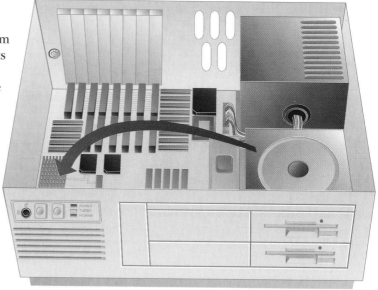

Running Application Programs

Once DOS is loaded, you can run other programs on your computer. These programs (called *applications*) allow your computer to do something useful, such as write letters, balance a checkbook, or play games.

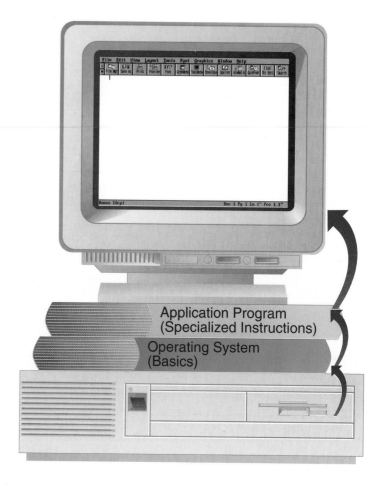

Application Program
(Specialized Instructions)

Operating System
(Basics)

What Happens When You Type?

When an application is running, you can use the keyboard and mouse to enter data into the computer and tell the computer what to do. The monitor echoes what is going on inside the system unit, so you can see what you or the computer are doing.

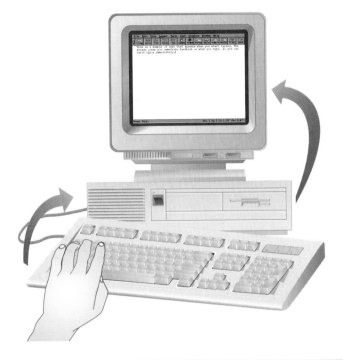

Saving Your Work

As you type data into the computer, the computer saves the data in its memory, which requires a constant flow of electricity. You must save the data from memory to a disk to have a permanent copy of the data.

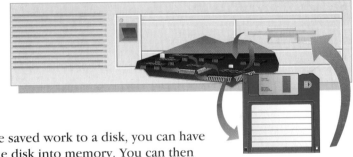

Retrieving Your Work

Once you have saved work to a disk, you can have the application retrieve the data from the disk into memory. You can then work with the data as needed.

LEARNING THE LINGO

BIOS: Pronounced "BUY-ose" and stands for basic input-output system. The BIOS consists of startup instructions and other instructions that tell the computer how to manage input (from the keyboard and mouse) and output (to the monitor and printer). The BIOS is stored in ROM.

CMOS: Sounds like "SEA-moss" and stands for complementary metal-oxide semiconductor. CMOS is battery-operated memory that keeps track of how many disk drives your computer has, today's date and time, and other useful information about your computer.

POST: Sounds like "post" and stands for power-on self test. Whenever you start your computer, the first thing it does is run a POST in order to determine whether the computer is functioning properly.

Application: A program that you can run after booting your computer. The application allows you to do useful tasks, such as writing letters and keeping an address book.

HOW A COMPUTER FUNCTIONS

How Does a Computer Think?

Although a computer's "brain" is much less complex than a human brain, it performs similar functions: it gathers data, processes the data, and creates some output. The way a computer does this, however, is very different, as you will see in the following descriptions.

Reading from a disk   Just as you might read instructions and information and then keep them in mind when performing a task, the system unit reads program instructions from disk into RAM. RAM stores the data and instructions so the central processing unit can quickly access it.

Receiving data from input devices In addition to reading instructions and data off disks, the system unit allows you to enter data and commands by using various input devices. For example, you can use a keyboard to type information into the computer or a joystick to play a game. Whatever you enter is stored in RAM, where the CPU can get at it.

Whenever you type a character on the keyboard, a unit of data called a *byte* is sent to the computer. A byte is an electrical representation of the character you typed.

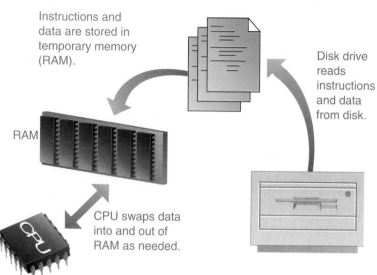

Instructions and data are stored in temporary memory (RAM).

RAM

Disk drive reads instructions and data from disk.

CPU swaps data into and out of RAM as needed.

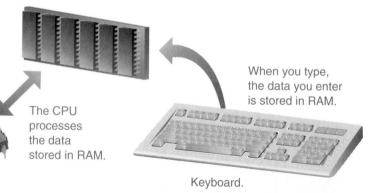

The CPU processes the data stored in RAM.

When you type, the data you enter is stored in RAM.

Keyboard.

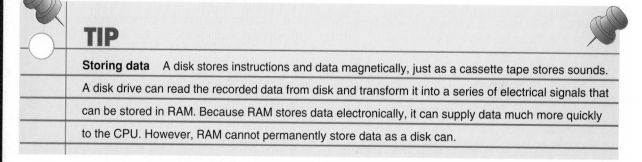

TIP

Storing data   A disk stores instructions and data magnetically, just as a cassette tape stores sounds.

A disk drive can read the recorded data from disk and transform it into a series of electrical signals that

can be stored in RAM. Because RAM stores data electronically, it can supply data much more quickly

to the CPU. However, RAM cannot permanently store data as a disk can.

Processing the data   Once the CPU has a set of instructions and some data, it can perform a task (for example, creating a graph or sorting a list of names in alphabetical order). As the CPU process data, it continuously swaps data and instructions into and out of RAM.

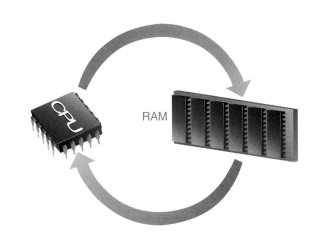

RAM

Outputting the data   As the CPU carries out a task, it echoes everything to the monitor, so you can see what is going on. This is one form of data output. Other forms of output include sounds, printed output, and (in some cases) faxes.

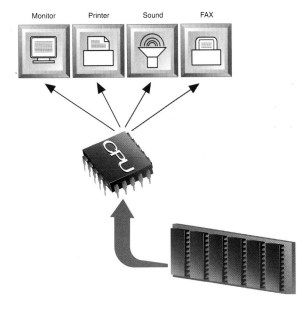

Monitor   Printer   Sound   FAX

Storing the data   As your computer processes data, the data is stored only electronically. To save the data permanently, you must store it on a disk. A disk stores the data magnetically, so when you turn the power off, the data is not lost.

LEARNING THE LINGO

Byte: A group of eight bits that usually represents a character or a number from 0 to 9. For example, the byte 01000001 represents the letter A. Each 0 or 1 in the byte is a *bit* (short for BInary digiT) representing one of two states: 0 for off or 1 for on. The various combinations of eight 0s and 1s represents all the data in a computer.

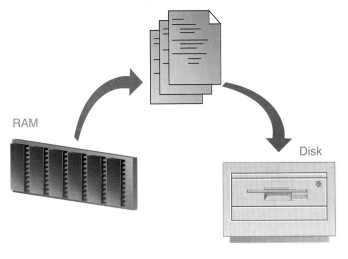

RAM

Disk

UNDERSTANDING MEMORY

Why Use Memory?

All computers need memory in order to store instructions and data in an electronic form that the computer can read and process quickly. All computers come with some memory, but the amount and types of memory can vary greatly from one computer to another.

Memory is measured in bytes, kilobytes, and megabytes. A byte is equivalent to one character. A kilobyte is 1,024 bytes. A megabyte is 1,024 kilobytes.

Types of Memory

Newer PCs come with at least one megabyte of memory.

Extended

Upper
(384k)

1 Megabyte

Conventional
(640k)

Extended memory is additional memory that acts just like conventional memory. Some computers come with additional memory, while others allow you to add memory later.

Upper memory is memory that is reserved for system use; for example, part of upper memory may be used to store the instructions for controlling a disk drive.

Conventional memory is the memory that comes with all IBM PCs and PC compatibles and is used for storing program instructions and data.

TIP

Extended memory requirements   In order for a computer to use extended memory, the computer must have an 80286 CPU or better and must have a program that manages extended memory. Such a program, called HIMEM.SYS, comes with DOS and Microsoft Windows.

Expanded memory is additional memory that swaps data into and out of conventional memory (640K RAM) at high speeds, giving the user the impression that the computer has more random-access memory (RAM) than the conventional 640K. Some programs are written to use expanded memory, allowing larger programs to run under DOS.

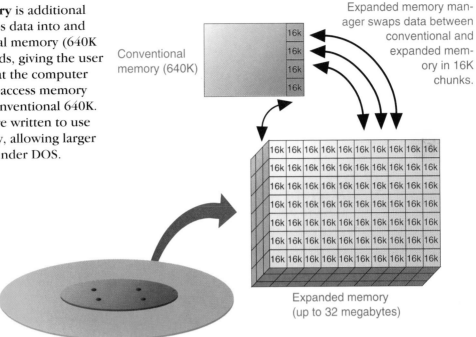

Conventional memory (640K)

Expanded memory manager swaps data between conventional and expanded memory in 16K chunks.

Expanded memory (up to 32 megabytes)

Where Does the Extra Memory Go?

The additional RAM chips can be installed directly on the motherboard or on a separate memory board that plugs into an expansion slot. Typically, RAM chips installed directly on the motherboard work faster and cost less to install.

SIMM   When you install memory, you usually plug a SIMM (single in-line memory module) into a memory slot on the motherboard. The SIMM contains one or more RAM chips.

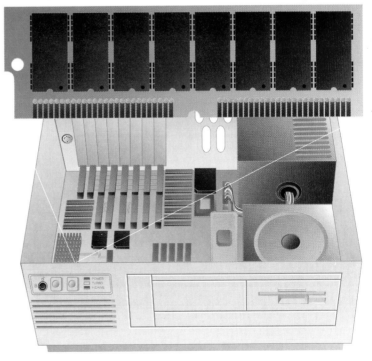

Quick Computer Tour

UNDERSTANDING MEMORY

How Much Memory Does Your Computer Have?

When you turn on your computer, it tests the memory to ensure that the RAM chips are operating properly. The test displays the amount of memory. So when you start your computer, keep an eye on the screen.

640K Base memory, 03072K Extended

Phoenix 80386 ROM BIOS PLUS
Copyright © 1985-1988 Phoenix Technologies Ltd.

640k Base Memory, 03072K Extended

TIP

Virtual memory   Some programs, including Microsoft Windows, allow you to use your disk drive to create additional memory. This memory is called *virtual memory*. Although it is slow (because it requires the computer to read data from disk), it does allow your computer to deal with larger files.

THE CENTRAL PROCESSING UNIT

What Does the CPU Do?

The central processing unit is the brain of your computer. It interprets the program instructions and processes the data you enter. CPUs are distinguished by three factors: the chip number, speed, and type.

Chip number   Each chip has a number (80286, 80386, 80486, and so on). In general, the higher the number, the more data the chip can process at one time. For example, a 286 chip can move 16 bits of data at one time, whereas a 386 chip can move 32 bits of data.

Chip speed   The chip speed is measured in megahertz (pronounced "MEG-a-hurts"). The higher the number, the faster the data is processed.

Chip type   The chip number is typically followed by an abbreviation that represents the chip type. SX indicates a step down from the original chip; SX chips are slower than normal. DX represents a step up from the SX. DX2 represents a step up from the DX.

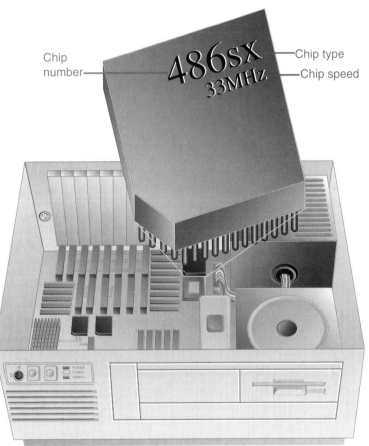

Chip number

Chip type

Chip speed

LEARNING THE LINGO

Data bus structure: The data bus structure determines how many bits of data the CPU can handle at one time. Think of the data bus as a highway. If the chip offers a 16-bit data bus, it is like a 16 lane highway. A chip that offers a 32-bit data bus is like a 32 lane highway and can handle much more data "traffic."

Chip: Another name for an integrated circuit. A chip is a silicon crystal or other material that is designed and manufactured to perform the same operations as hundreds, thousands, or millions of electronic components (transistors, resistors, and so on). A "large" chip may be the size of your fingernail.

Quick Computer Tour

THE CENTRAL PROCESSING UNIT

Boosting CPU Performance with Cache Memory

Some CPUs come with built-in cache memory that can decrease the amount of time the CPU spends getting data from RAM.

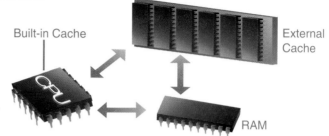

Built-in Cache Memory is super-fast memory that is built into the CPU. The CPU stores commonly used instructions and data in the cache, to cut down on the number of times it has to swap data into and out of RAM.

Built-in Cache

External Cache

RAM

External Cache Memory is additional memory that works faster than RAM but slower than the built-in cache. External cache memory comes in the form of SRAM (static random-access memory chips).

Upgrading a CPU

In some computers, you can increase the speed of the computer by installing a faster chip. On other systems, you can boost the performance of the existing CPU.

Upgradable CPUs   Some CPUs come with a vacancy socket that allows you to plug in an additional performance-boosting CPU later.

Math Coprocessors   A math coprocessor is a chip that specializes in performing complex mathematical calculations. If you use a program that supports a math coprocessor, you may be able to boost performance by up to 500%.

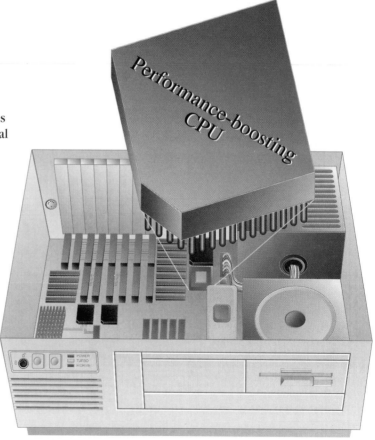

Performance-boosting CPU

PART 2

Input and Output Devices

If you had a brain but no way to take in information or do anything useful, your brain would be useless. Similarly, a system unit without any input and output devices would be a worthless piece of equipment. In this part, you will learn about the various devices that allow you to communicate with the system unit and produce output.

- Using a Keyboard
- Using a Mouse
- Using a Joystick
- Watching the Monitor
- Seeing Your Work in Print
- Communicating over the Phone with Modems
- Scanners and What They Do
- Wiring Your Computer for Sound

USING A KEYBOARD

What Is a Keyboard?

The keyboard contains the keys you use to type data into the computer and enter commands. Although the *locations* of the keys on your keyboard may differ from the one shown here, your keyboard should contain the same keys.

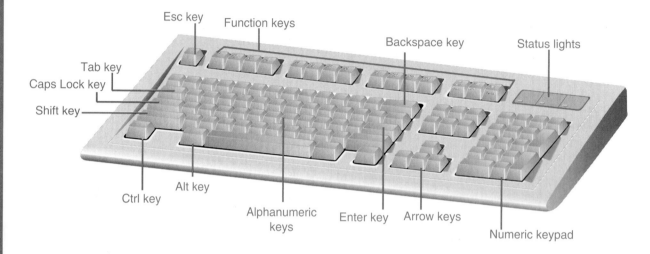

Alphanumeric keys *Alphanumeric* is a fancy term for "letters and numbers." These are the keys you use for typing and entering data.

Shift key Hold down the **Shift** key while typing a character to make the character uppercase.

Caps Lock key Press and release the **Caps Lock** key to make all characters you type uppercase. Press and release the key again to turn Caps Lock off.

Enter key Use the **Enter** key to end a paragraph in a word-processing program or to confirm or execute a command you selected or typed.

Tab key Use the **Tab** key to indent the first line in a paragraph of text or to move from one area of the screen to another.

Backspace key The backspace key deletes any characters to the left of the cursor one-by-one.

Function keys Function keys typically are used to enter commands quickly. For example, in most programs, you can press the **F1** key to display help. On some keyboards, the function keys are located on the left side of the keyboard.

Arrow keys Also known as cursor-movement keys, the arrow keys move the cursor (the blinking line or box) around on-screen.

Numeric keypad   The numeric keypad consists of a group of number keys arranged like the keys on an adding machine. This keypad includes a Num Lock key. With Num Lock off, you use the numeric keypad to move around on-screen. With Num Lock on, you use the keypad to type numbers.

Ctrl and Alt keys   The Ctrl (Control) and Alt (Alternative) keys make the other keys on the keyboard act differently from the way they normally act. For example, if you press the F1 key by itself, the computer may display a help screen, but if you hold down the Ctrl key while pressing F1, the computer will carry out an entirely different command.

Esc key   You can use the Esc (Escape) key in most programs to back out of or quit whatever you are currently doing.

Status lights   The status lights show whether Num Lock or Caps Lock is on (status light on) or off (status light off).

TIP

Typing aids   Many keyboards have a fold-out stand in front that you can pull down to tilt the keyboard. Tilting the keyboard often makes it easier to reach the keys.

If your typing skills are getting a little rusty, you can purchase a typing program for your computer. A typing program leads you through the basics, provides exercise sessions, tests your accuracy and speed, and drills you on the keys with which you are having the most trouble. One of the better typing programs on the market is Typing Tutor. Typing Tutor even includes an arcade game that can help you hone your typing skills while you play.

Input and Output Devices

USING A MOUSE

Do You Need a Mouse?

Although the keyboard allows you to move around on the screen and enter commands and text, it's fairly stiff as far as control mechanisms go. A mouse allows you to move more smoothly and quickly around the screen.

The Mouse and Its Pointer

If you have a mouse and a program that *supports* (allows you to use) a mouse, a mouse pointer will appear on-screen when you start the program. The appearance of the pointer varies depending on the program.

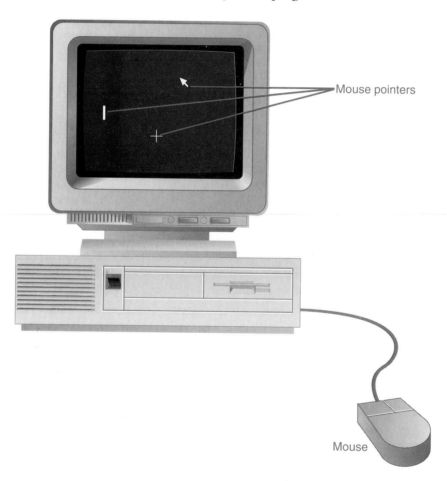

Mouse pointers

Mouse

As you roll the mouse around on your desk (or on a mouse pad), the pointer moves on-screen in the same direction. You can take the following actions with the mouse:

Point   Slide the mouse on your desk until the tip of the mouse pointer is touching the desired item. When you point, nothing happens until you press the mouse button.

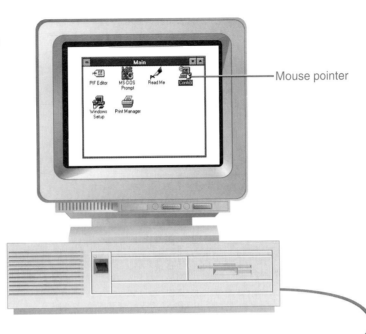

Mouse pointer

Click   Once you have pointed to something, you can select it by *clicking* (pressing and releasing) the mouse button. You will usually use the left mouse button.

Double-click   To enter a command or activate the item you are pointing to, quickly press and release the mouse button twice without moving the mouse.

Click

23

USING A MOUSE

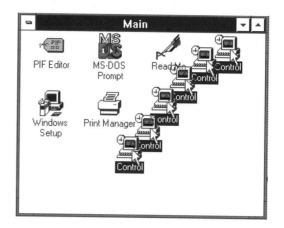

Drag To drag an item on the screen, point to it, and hold down the mouse button while sliding the mouse on your desk. You usually drag to select letters or words, move something on-screen, or draw a line or shape.

Controlling Your Mouse

Most programs allow you to change the mouse settings to make the mouse behave the way you want.

You can change the speed at which the pointer moves.

You can change the double-click interval.

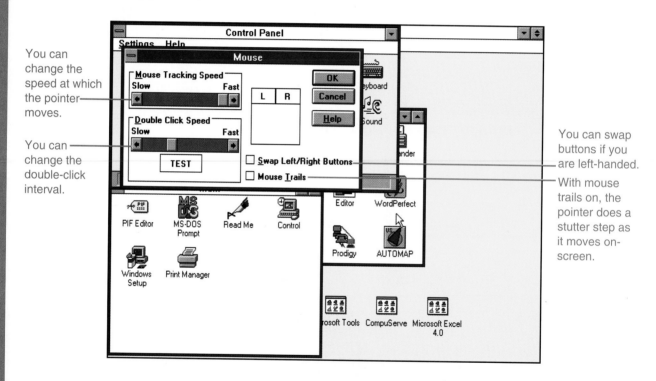

You can swap buttons if you are left-handed.

With mouse trails on, the pointer does a stutter step as it moves on-screen.

TIP

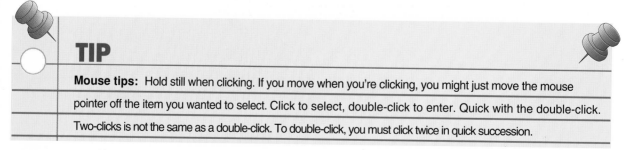

Mouse tips: Hold still when clicking. If you move when you're clicking, you might just move the mouse pointer off the item you wanted to select. Click to select, double-click to enter. Quick with the double-click.

Two-clicks is not the same as a double-click. To double-click, you must click twice in quick succession.

USING A JOYSTICK

What Is a Joystick?

A joystick looks a little bit like a stick shift lever on a car, and gives you greater control when you use your computer to play arcade games.

Greater control   If you don't have a joystick, you must use the arrow keys to move up, down, left, or right. With a joystick, you move the stick in any direction you want to move, even on an angle.

Buttons
The joystick buttons allow you to enter commands, such as Drop Bomb or Shoot Missile.

Connecting a Joystick

The joystick plugs into a game port on the back of your computer.

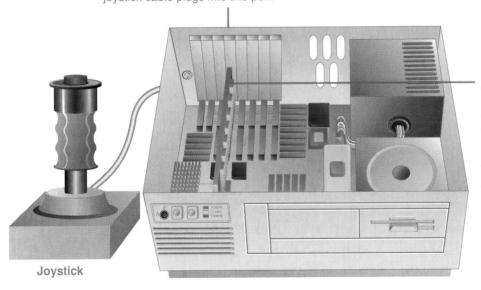

Game port   The joystick card has a game port that sticks out the back of the system unit. The joystick cable plugs into this port.

Joystick card
If your computer does not have a game port, you must purchase a joystick card and plug it into one of the expansion slots inside the system unit.

Joystick

WATCHING THE MONITOR

What Is a Monitor?

A monitor is a lot like a high-quality television set. As you work, the monitor lets you see what you are doing. The video adapter and monitor work together to display information.

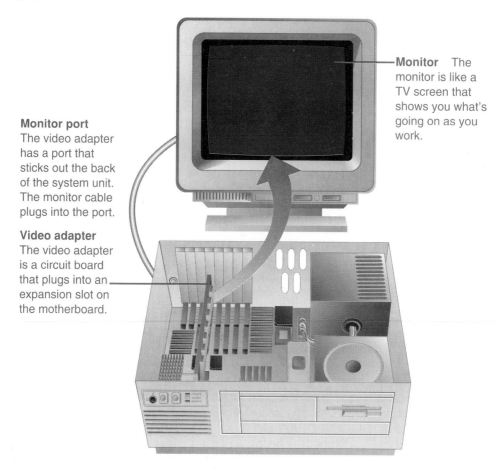

Monitor The monitor is like a TV screen that shows you what's going on as you work.

Monitor port
The video adapter has a port that sticks out the back of the system unit. The monitor cable plugs into the port.

Video adapter
The video adapter is a circuit board that plugs into an expansion slot on the motherboard.

Types of Video Adapters and Monitors

Video adapters and monitors are distinguished by two qualities: color (or black-and-white) and resolution.

Color monitors are like color TVs. However, some color monitors can display more colors than others. Most color monitors display 16 or 256 colors. More advanced monitors can display up to 16.7 million colors.

Monochrome display   Color display

Resolution is measured by the number or dots or *pixels* that the screen displays. The more pixels (or dots per inch, dpi), the clearer the image.

CGA (Color Graphics Adapter) Displays one color in 200 by 640 dpi (dots per inch) or four colors in 200 by 320 dpi. CGA monitors are obsolete.

EGA (Enhanced Graphics Adapter) A step up from CGA. It can display 16 colors simultaneously in a resolution of 350 by 640 dpi. EGA monitors are obsolete.

VGA (Video Graphics Array) Available in three forms: VGA, Enhanced VGA, and Super VGA. VGA displays 256 colors with a resolution of 640 by 480 dpi. Enhanced VGA offers higher resolution: 800 by 600 dpi. Super VGA offers the highest resolution: 1024 by 768 dpi.

Input and Output Devices

WATCHING THE MONITOR

Video adapter features   In addition to color and high-resolution, many video adapters come with built-in memory and an accelerator. The more memory an adapter has, the more colors it can display. Video memory can come in two forms: as RAM chips or VRAM (Video RAM) chips. VRAM chips are faster but cost more.

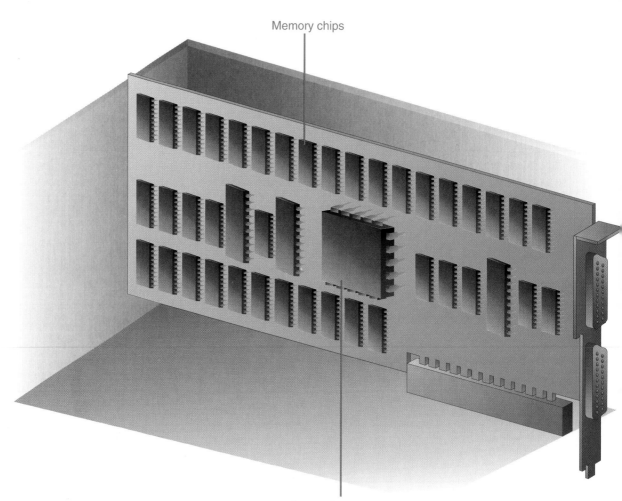

Memory chips

An accelerator can help the screen display images more quickly.

SEEING YOUR WORK IN PRINT

Why Print?

After you have created a letter or some other document, you can enter a command to have the document sent to your printer. The printer converts your document from its electronic form into a printout that you can use just as if you had created the document on a typewriter.

Types of Printers

There are three types of printers: dot-matrix, laser, and inkjet.

Dot-matrix printers create characters and lines as patterns of tiny dots. Dot matrix printers are inexpensive, but they are loud, slow, and produce low-quality print.

A dot-matrix printer typically comes with a tractor feed mechanism that pulls continuous form paper into the printer.

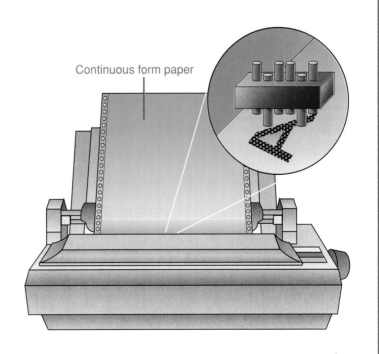

Continuous form paper

29

SEEING YOUR WORK IN PRINT

Laser printers work like photocopy machines and produce high-quality printouts. Although laser printers are expensive, they are quiet and fast.

A laser printer comes with a paper tray that feeds blank sheets of paper into the printer one at a time.

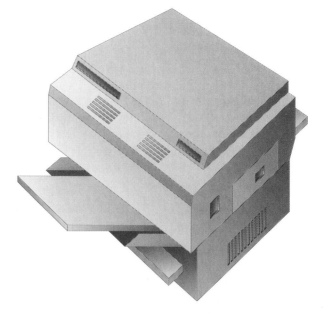

Inkjet printers create characters and lines by spraying ink on the paper. Inkjet printers are less expensive than laser printers and are typically slower, but they are quiet and produce high-quality printouts.

As with a laser printer, an inkjet printer feeds individual pages into the printer.

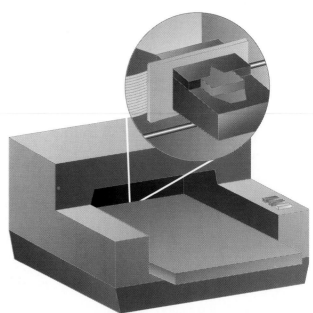

TIP

Quality and speed   Printers are usually compared by the quality of print and the speed at which they print. Quality is measured in dpi (dots per inch); in general, the more dots per inch, the higher the quality. Speed is measured in CPS (characters per second) or PPM (pages per minute).

Controlling the Printer

Although every printer has several buttons that allow you to select different type styles, sizes, and print quality, you will control the printer mostly from the program you used to create your document.

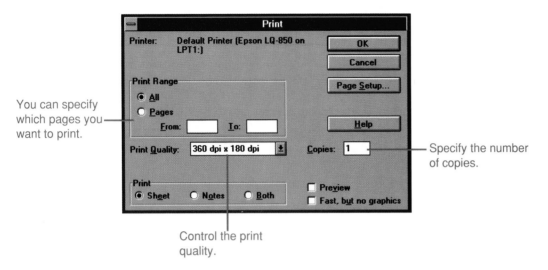

You can specify which pages you want to print.

Control the print quality.

Specify the number of copies.

Online indicator light Before you can print a document, you must have paper in the printer, the printer must be on, and the online indicator light must be lit (not flashing). If the online light is not lit, the printer is not ready to print. Check to see if the printer has paper, and then press the **Online** button.

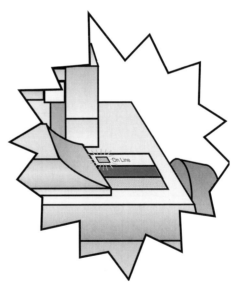

Input and Output Devices

COMMUNICATING OVER THE PHONE WITH MODEMS

What Does a Modem Do?

A modem allows your computer to communicate with another computer across town or in another state or country.

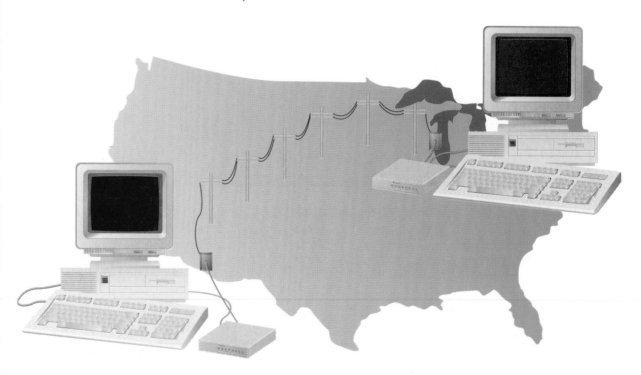

Modem stands for MOdulator/DEModulator. When you send data, the modem modulates the computer signal, changing it to a form that can be sent over the phone lines (an analog signal).

When an incoming signal reaches the modem, the modem translates the signal into a form that the computer can understand (a digital signal).

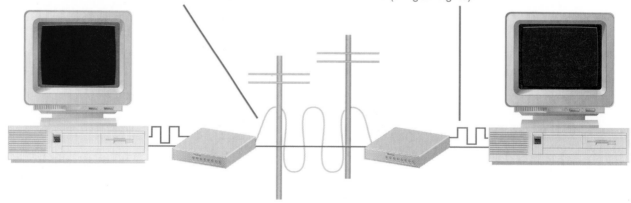

LEARNING THE LINGO

Bits per second (bps): Commonly confused with *baud rate*. Baud is a measure of the number of changes in an electrical signal per second. During high-speed data transfers, a modem may send more than one bit of information for each change in the electrical signal. For example, a modem operating at 300 baud may be transferring at 1,200 bps.

Types of Modems

You can get a modem that fits inside your computer (internal modem) or one that plugs into a port on the back of the system unit (external modem).

Internal modem is a card that snaps into an expansion slot on the motherboard. You plug a phone line into the jack on the card.

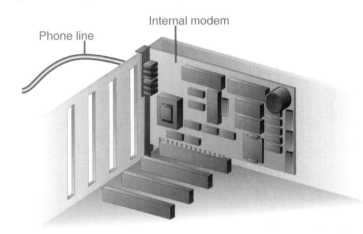

External modem is a box that sits outside the computer. You plug a phone line into the modem, plug the modem into a power source, and connect the modem to the system unit with a serial cable.

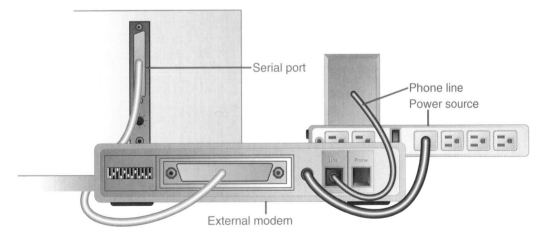

Speed Modems are distinguished by the speed at which they send and receive data. Speed is measured in bps (bits per second). When transferring data, both modems must communicate at the same speed.

Input and Output Devices

COMMUNICATING OVER THE PHONE WITH MODEMS

Data compression   To increase the speed at which data is transferred, some modems automatically compress data before sending it and decompress data when they receive it. The compression feature squeezes data so it takes fewer signals to send the same data.

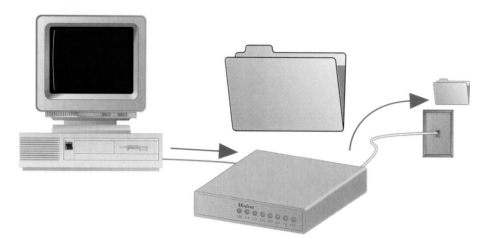

What You Can Do with a Modem

Because a modem connects you to the phone line, it allows you to reach out with your computer to other computers and services.

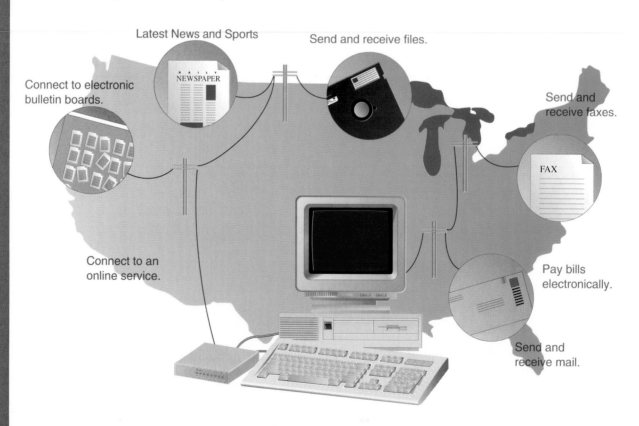

Latest News and Sports

Send and receive files.

Connect to electronic bulletin boards.

Send and receive faxes.

Connect to an online service.

Pay bills electronically.

Send and receive mail.

TIP

Busy signal: When you are using your modem, that phone line will be busy if anyone tries to call you. Likewise, if you dial a long-distance phone number with your modem, you will be charged long-distance rates.

LEARNING THE LINGO

Compression standards: Both modems must use the same compression standards. Common compression standards are:

MNP5   Compresses a file to half its size.

CCITT V.42bis   Compresses a file to a quarter of its size.

A 2,400 bps modem using V.42bis data compression can transfer data at a rate of 9,600 bps.

Input and Output Devices

SCANNERS AND WHAT THEY DO

What Is a Scanner?

A scanner is sort of like a copy machine. However, instead of copying a page to another piece of paper, the scanner copies it to your computer's memory.

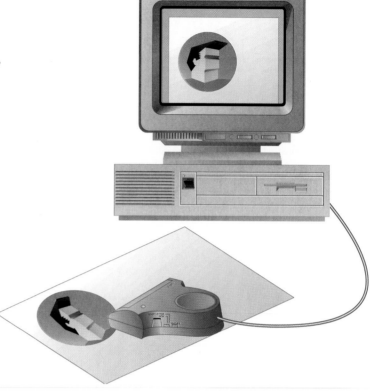

Saving the image on disk Once you have scanned an image, you can save it in a file on disk.

Pasting the image into documents Because the image is in a separate file, you can paste the image into your documents, just as if the image were a piece of clip art.

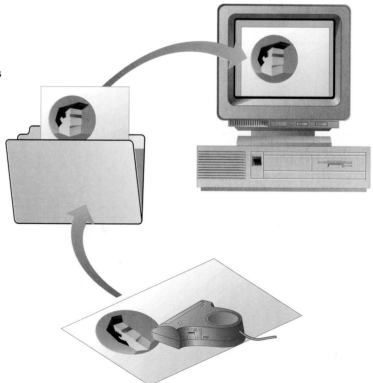

Optical character recognition (OCR)   In addition to pictures, some scanners allow you to scan text. Special software converts the text from patterns of dots into characters. You can then open the file in a word-processing program and edit the text.

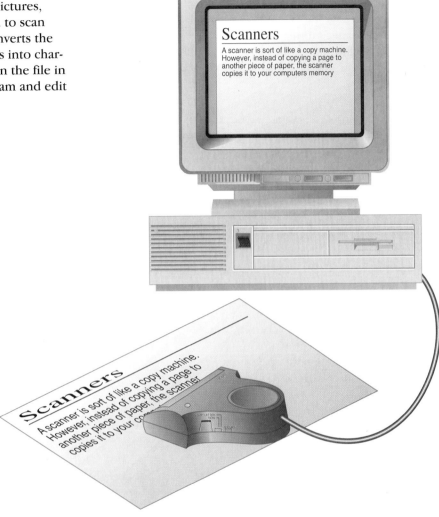

Types of Scanners

Scanners come in two types: hand-held and flatbed.

Hand-held scanners   With a hand-held scanner, you drag the scanner across the page. To scan the image clearly, you must have a steady hand. Hand-held scanners are good for scanning photos and small pieces of art.

Input and Output Devices

SCANNERS AND WHAT THEY DO

Flatbed scanners   Flatbed scanners work like copy machines. You place the page you want to scan face down on the scanner, and it scans the page automatically.

Color scanners   Some scanners can scan images in color (usually 16 or 256 colors). Others scan only in black, white, and gray. If you have only a black-and-white printer, a color scanner won't do you much good.

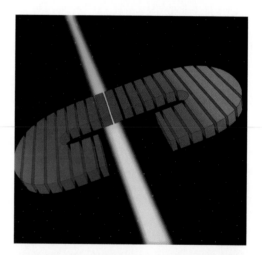

Gray scales   A black-and-white scanner can usually scan various shades of gray. The number of shades a scanner can distinguish is called the *gray scale*. Most scanners can scan up to 256 shades of gray.

Resolution   Most scanners have several settings that allow you to scan with more or less detail. At 100 dots per inch, an image will appear with little detail. At 400 dots per inch, you can see more details.

WIRING YOUR COMPUTER FOR SOUND

Why Increase Your Computer's Sound Quality?

Every computer comes with a speaker that can emit beeps and robotic-sounding voices, but if you want to hear music and cool sound effects, you must install a sound board.

The sound board slides into an expansion slot inside the system unit.

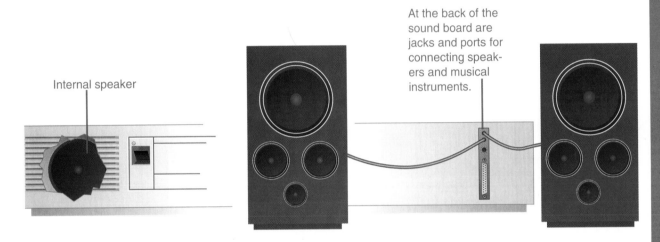

At the back of the sound board are jacks and ports for connecting speakers and musical instruments.

Internal speaker

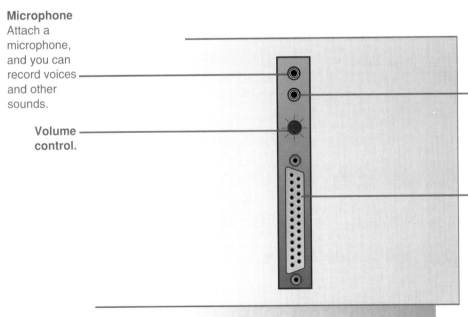

Microphone
Attach a microphone, and you can record voices and other sounds.

Volume control.

Speakers or amplifier You can plug in a set of speakers or connect the sound board to the input jack on your home stereo.

MIDI interface The MIDI (Musical Instrument Digital Interface) lets you connect a musical instrument or synthesizer to the sound board. You can then record, save, edit, and play back music and other sounds.

39

WIRING YOUR COMPUTER FOR SOUND

Sound effects Although you can use a sound board to record and play back voices, music, and other sounds, most people install a sound board so they can hear the nifty sound effects created by their favorite computer games.

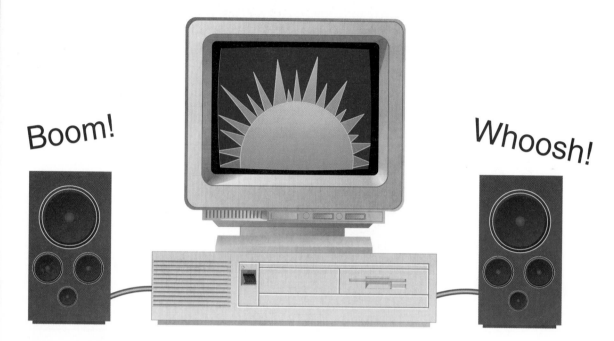

Boom!

Whoosh!

TIP

Special software If you plan on using your sound board to record and play back sounds and music, you will need specialized software. Some sound boards come with the basic software you need, but you can purchase more sophisticated software depending on your needs.

PART 3

Where Is the Data Stored?

When your computer is following program instructions and processing data, the instructions and data are in electronic form. When the electricity stops flowing, the data is gone. Because of this, the computer needs permanent data storage in the form of disks. In this part, you will learn how a computer stores data, and you will learn about the various storage devices.

- Understanding Data Storage
- Floppy Disk Drives
- Hard Disk Drives
- CD-ROM Drives

UNDERSTANDING DATA STORAGE

How a Computer Stores Data

A computer stores data in much the same way as a cassette player stores sounds on a tape—magnetically.

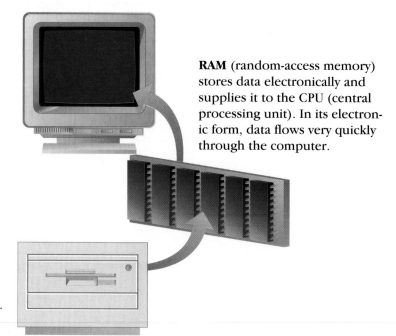

RAM (random-access memory) stores data electronically and supplies it to the CPU (central processing unit). In its electronic form, data flows very quickly through the computer.

Disks store data permanently, in a magnetic form. When you tell the computer to retrieve data, the disk drive reads the data in its magnetic form and converts it to an electronic form.

Understanding Disks, Directories, and Files

Whenever you type a document or create something on the computer, you should save your work permanently in a *file* on a *disk*.

File   A *file* is like a folder that you might use to store a report or a letter. You name the file, so you can later find and retrieve the information it contains.

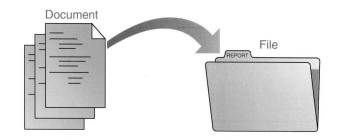

Document

File

REPORT

TIP

Specifying a Disk Drive When you tell the computer to look at a specific drive, you must specify the drive's letter followed by a colon. For example, to change to drive C, you type **c:**.

Disks Files are stored on *disks*. Your computer probably has a *hard disk* inside it (called drive C) to which you can save your files. You can also save files to *floppy disks*, which you insert into the slots (the floppy disk drives) on the front of the computer (drives A and B).

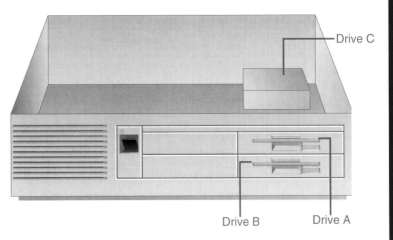

Drive C

Drive B   Drive A

Directories To keep files organized on a disk, you can create *directories* on the disk. Each directory acts as a drawer in a filing cabinet, storing a group of related files. Although you can create directories on both floppy and hard disks, most people use directories only on hard disks.

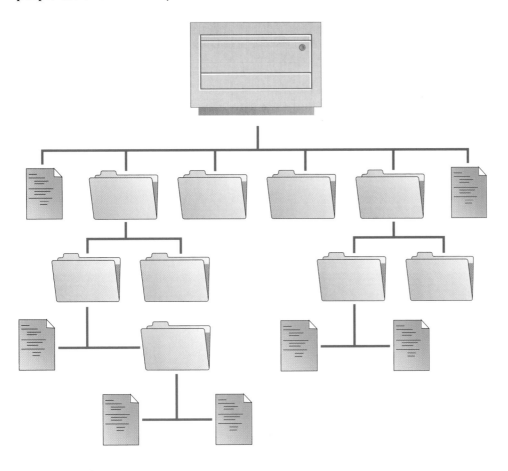

Where Is the Data Stored?

UNDERSTANDING DATA STORAGE

Naming Files

Whenever you save a file to disk, you must name the file and indicate the disk and directory where you want the file stored.

Path specifies the directory in which you want to save the file.

Period separates the file name and extension.

`C:\data\letters\bill01.doc`

Drive letter indicates the disk drive where you want the file saved.

File name can be up to eight characters long.

Extension is optional and can be up to three characters long. The extension usually indicates the type of file (in this case, document).

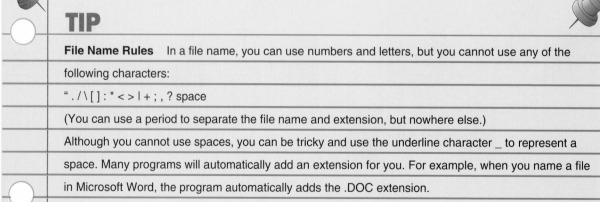

C:

\WINDOWS   \DOS   \DATA

\FONT

\SYSTEM

\TEMP

\PERSONAL

\LETTERS

\QUOTES

bill01.doc

TIP

File Name Rules   In a file name, you can use numbers and letters, but you cannot use any of the following characters:

" . / \ [ ] : * < > | + ; , ? space

(You can use a period to separate the file name and extension, but nowhere else.)

Although you cannot use spaces, you can be tricky and use the underline character _ to represent a space. Many programs will automatically add an extension for you. For example, when you name a file in Microsoft Word, the program automatically adds the .DOC extension.

FLOPPY DISK DRIVES

What Are Floppy Disk Drives?

The drives on the front of the system unit are the floppy disk drives. They come in two sizes, 5.25-inch and 3.5-inch.

5.25-inch drive   A 5.25-inch drive can use 5.25-inch disks. You insert the disk as shown (label side up), and then close the drive door or flip the lever down.

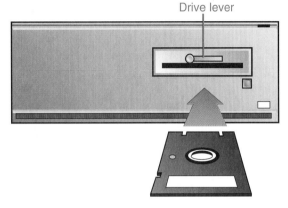

Drive lever

3.5-inch drive   A 3.5-inch drive uses 3.5-inch disks. You insert the disk as shown. To remove the disk, press the eject button.

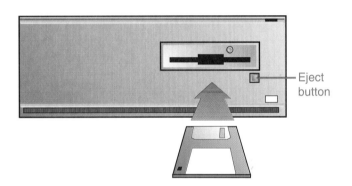

Eject button

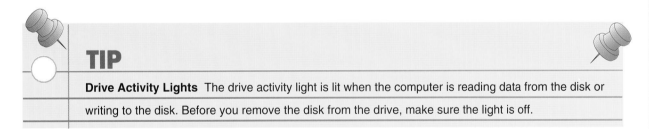

TIP

Drive Activity Lights   The drive activity light is lit when the computer is reading data from the disk or writing to the disk. Before you remove the disk from the drive, make sure the light is off.

Where Is the Data Stored?

FLOPPY DISK DRIVES

Types of Floppy Disks

Floppy disks differ not only in physical size, but also in respect to capacity (how much data the disks can store).

Capacity   Capacity is measured in kilobytes (about one thousand bytes) and megabytes (about one million bytes). Common disk sizes and capacities are listed in the table.

Density is a measure of how much data can be crammed on a disk in a given amount of space. A high-density disk uses smaller magnetic particles to store each piece of data. This allows a high-density disk to store more data in less space than a double-density disk.

Disk Size	Disk Type	Capacity
5.25-inch	Double-density	360 kilobytes
5.25-inch	High-density	1.2 megabytes
3.5-inch	Double-density	720 kilobytes
3.5-inch	High-density	1.44 megabytes

Double-density

High-density

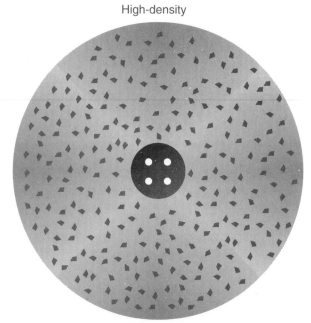

TIP

High-capacity drives   Most new disk drives are high-capacity drives; they can handle both high-density and double-density disks. Older drives were low-capacity drives and could handle only double-density disks.

Preparing Disks to Store Data

Before you can use a floppy disk, the disk must be *formatted*. You can buy formatted disks or buy disks and format them yourself.

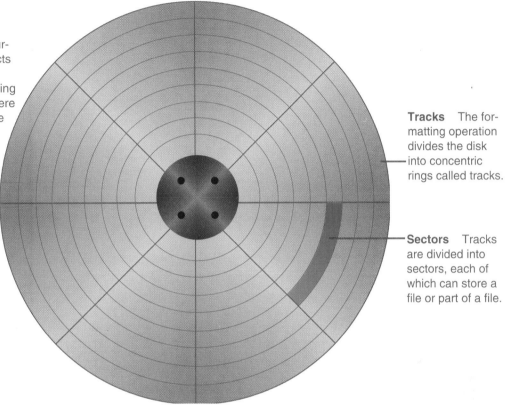

A **file-allocation table** (created during formatting) acts as a classroom seating chart, telling the computer where all the sectors are located.

Tracks   The formatting operation divides the disk into concentric rings called tracks.

Sectors   Tracks are divided into sectors, each of which can store a file or part of a file.

TIP

Formatting Formatting a disk is easy. You stick it in the floppy disk drive and enter the Format command. The operating system and the computer do the rest. You will learn how to format a disk in the next part of this book.

LEARNING THE LINGO

Format: Formatting organizes the storage areas on disk so data can be stored in known locations.

Tracks: A track on a computer disk is similar to a groove in a phonograph record. However, unlike the groove in a phonograph record, which is one continuous spiral, each track on a disk is a separate ring.

Sectors: A sector is a division of a track. Each sector can store a file or a part of a file.

Where Is the Data Stored?

HARD DISK DRIVES

What Is a Hard Disk?

Most new computers have a hard disk drive inside the computer. The hard disk drive is like a giant floppy disk drive that has a nonremovable disk.

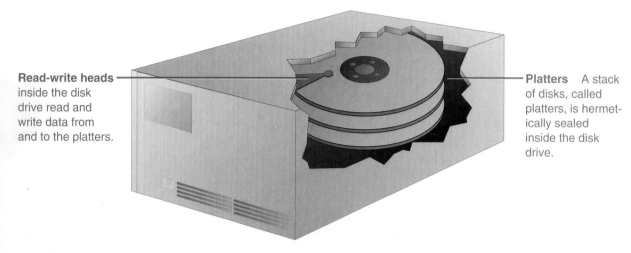

Read-write heads inside the disk drive read and write data from and to the platters.

Platters A stack of disks, called platters, is hermetically sealed inside the disk drive.

Hard Disk Size and Speed

Hard disk drives vary in the amount of data they can store and in the speed at which they can read data from disks.

Capacity An 80-megabyte hard disk drive can store roughly the same amount of data that can be stored on sixty-six 5.25-inch high-density disks or fifty-five 3.5-inch high-density disks.

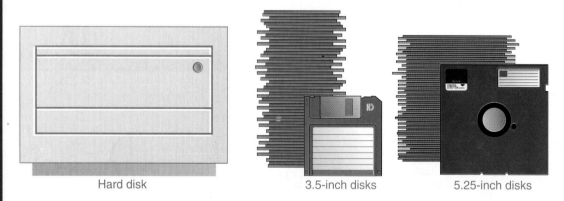

Hard disk   3.5-inch disks   5.25-inch disks

Speed The speed at which a hard disk can retrieve a piece of data is measured in milliseconds (1/1000 of a second) and is called the *average access time*. Most hard disk drives have an average access time between 15 and 20 milliseconds.

Hard disk drives are also distinguished by the way they are connected to the system unit. The two most common hard disk drives are the *IDE* and the *SCSI*.

Speeding Up Your Disk with a Disk Cache

You can increase the speed at which your computer gets data by using a *disk cache*. A *disk cache* is a portion of a computer's electronic memory that is set aside to hold frequently used data. DOS and Windows both come with a disk caching program called SMARTdrive that creates and manages the cache for you. All you have to do is run the program.

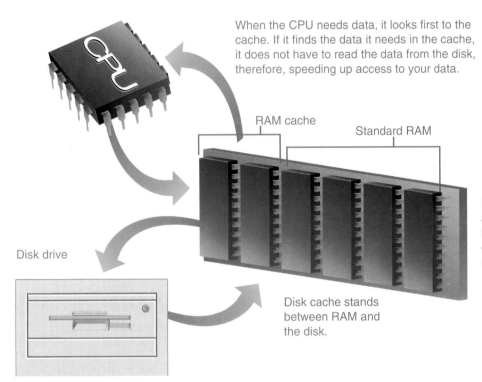

When the CPU needs data, it looks first to the cache. If it finds the data it needs in the cache, it does not have to read the data from the disk, therefore, speeding up access to your data.

RAM cache

Standard RAM

Recently accessed data is stored in the cache, where it is readily available.

Disk drive

Disk cache stands between RAM and the disk.

LEARNING THE LINGO

IDE (intelligent drive electronics) controller: Most computers come with an IDE drive and connector that connects the drive directly to the motherboard.

SCSI (small computer system interface) controller: A SCSI (pronounced "SCUZZ-y") controller is a card that plugs into an expansion slot on the motherboard. A high-performance SCSI hard disk can plug into the card along with several other SCSI devices. SCSI hard drives are fast, powerful, and expensive.

CD-ROM DRIVES

What Is a CD-ROM Drive?

A CD-ROM drive uses the same kind of disks you play in an audio CD player. Instead of music, CD-ROM disks store computer files and programs. A single disk can store over 650 megabytes of information, which is almost equivalent to a complete set of encyclopedias.

Headphone jack Allows you to plug in a set of headphones and listen to any sounds that are recorded on disk.

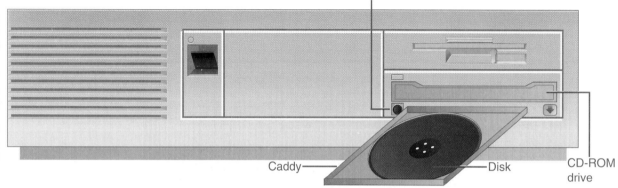

Caddy Disk CD-ROM drive

To insert the disk, you normally place the disk in a caddy and then slide the caddy into the drive.

Laser technology Unlike floppy disks and hard disks, which store data in a magnetic form, compact disks store data using microscopic pits on the surface of the disk. A tiny laser inside the disk drive bounces light off the disk to read the recorded data.

Mega-storage CD-ROM disks are commonly used for storing encyclopedias, books, and catalogues, complete with text, full-color photos and illustrations, and sounds. Because this information is computerized, you can have the computer search for specific data much more quickly than you could by hand.

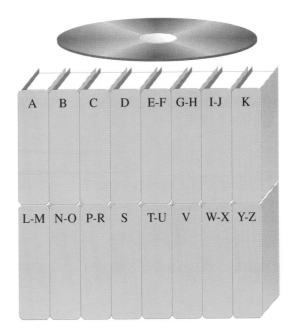

Sounds and movies CD-ROM disks often include sounds, pictures, and movie clips. The CD-ROM player may work through a sound board or allow you to attach headphones in order to listen to the recorded sounds.

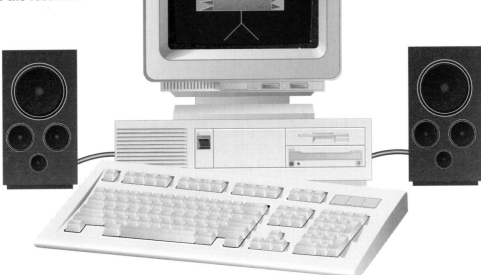

Because CD-ROM disks can store text, graphics, animation sequences, movie clips, voices, music, and other data, CD-ROM technology is essential when it comes to creating or playing multimedia presentations. Multimedia combines text, video, graphics, and animation for use in presentations and training.

Where Is the Data Stored?

PART 4

Working with DOS and Windows

In order to do anything useful, your computer needs a set of instructions that tell it what to do. The most basic form of instructions is the *operating system*. You commonly will use the operating system to view a list of files, copy files, and run other programs. In this part, you will learn how to work with the most popular operating system—MS-DOS, and a graphical environment, called Microsoft Windows, that runs on top of DOS.

- Booting Your Computer with DOS
- Entering Commands at the DOS Prompt
- Changing to a Disk Drive
- Changing to a Directory
- Making and Deleting Directories
- Displaying a List of Files
- Formatting a Floppy Disk
- Copying Files

- Deleting Files
- Using the DOS Shell
- Working with Dialog Boxes
- Working with Microsoft Windows
- Selecting Commands from Pull-Down Menus
- Responding to Dialog Boxes
- Controlling Windows

BOOTING YOUR COMPUTER WITH DOS

What Is Booting?

Before you can use your computer, you must turn it on with the operating system (usually DOS) in place. This procedure is called *booting*. Most computers now come with a hard disk (inside the computer) that already has DOS on it. The following steps assume DOS is on your computer's hard disk.

TIP

Power strip If all the parts of your computer are plugged into a power strip, you can turn everything on from the power strip. Just leave the switches on the monitor, system unit, and printer in the On position. You can then turn the computer on or off simply by flipping the power switch on the strip.

Turning On Your Computer

1. Remove all floppy disks from the floppy disk drives.

2. Make sure all your computer equipment is properly connected and is plugged in. If all your computer equipment is plugged into a power strip, flip the switch on the power strip to turn it on.

3. Flip the power switch, or press the power button on the monitor to turn it on.

4. Flip the power switch, or press the power button on the system unit to turn it on.

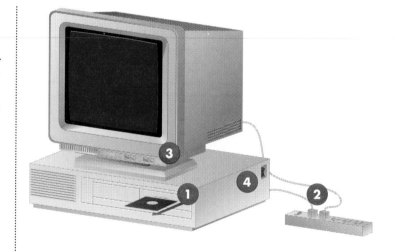

Rebooting Your Computer

If your computer locks up (stops responding when you press keys or move your mouse), you may need to reboot it by performing the following steps:

1 Hold down the **Ctrl** key and the **Alt** key (**Ctrl+Alt**).

2 Press the **Del** key.

3 Release the Ctrl, Alt, and Del keys.

Resetting Your Computer

If your computer refuses to reboot, look for a Reset button on the front of the system unit. If you find a Reset button, press and release it to reboot your computer.

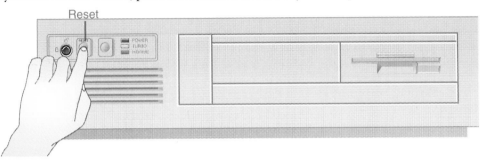

TIP

Blank screen? If your screen is blank, make sure the monitor is on. If the monitor is on, try cranking up the brightness and contrast.

LEARNING THE LINGO

Operating system: An operating system is a set of basic instructions that control the overall operations of your computer, such as saving data to disk. The two most common operating systems are DOS and OS/2. This book focuses on DOS.

DOS: DOS stands for Disk Operating System, the most common operating system in use today.

Boot: To turn on your computer with the operating system instructions in place (on a disk in one of your computer's disk drives).

Reboot or warm boot: When you reboot your computer (by pressing **Ctrl+Alt+Del**), the computer rereads the disk operating system without turning the power off and then on to the computer.

Working with DOS and Windows

ENTERING COMMANDS AT THE DOS PROMPT

What Is the DOS Prompt?

After you boot your computer, you will see the DOS prompt on-screen. This prompt is DOS's way of showing you that it is ready to accept a command. You will type commands at the DOS prompt to run a program or perform some other task (such as change disk drives, view lists, or copy files).

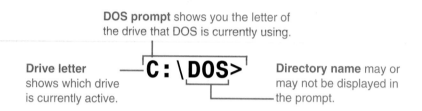

DOS prompt shows you the letter of the drive that DOS is currently using.

Drive letter shows which drive is currently active.

Directory name may or may not be displayed in the prompt.

Typing a Command at the DOS Prompt

When the DOS prompt is displayed, you can enter a command at the prompt to tell DOS what task you want it to perform. For example, you might take the following steps to copy a file from one disk to another:

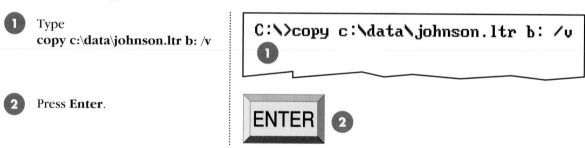

1 Type
copy c:\data\johnson.ltr b: /v

2 Press **Enter**.

Although many DOS commands can consist of merely one part (the command itself), some contain additional elements that give DOS specific instructions on how to execute the command. This picture illustrates the various parts of a DOS command line.

Command Tells DOS which action you want DOS to carry out.

Delimiters Spaces and special characters that break down the command line for DOS.

DOS prompt You type the command next to the DOS prompt. You do NOT type the prompt.

```
C:\>copy c:\data\johnson.ltr b: /v
```

Parameters Specify the objects on which you want DOS to perform the action. For example, if you tell DOS to copy a file, you must specify which file or files you want it to copy and where you want the copies placed.

Switches Allow you to control how the command performs its action. The /V switch tells DOS to verify the copy operation.

When you type a DOS command, you must follow the proper syntax (order) for the command. For example, you must type the command first.

LEARNING THE LINGO

Syntax: The order in which you must type the elements that make up the command line. Type the command first, then the parameters, and then the switches. To learn the correct syntax for a command, type the command followed by a space and the **/?** switch, and then press **Enter**.

TIP

Uppercase or lowercase? When you type a DOS command, you can use uppercase characters, lowercase characters, or a mix of the two. DOS does not distinguish between uppercase and lowercase characters; to DOS, COPY, copy, and cOpY are all the same command.

Exercise

The following exercise will give you some practice with entering harmless DOS commands.

1 Type **c:** and press **Enter**.

2 Type **prompt pg** and press **Enter**.

3 Type **cd\dos** and press **Enter**.

4 Type **date** and press **Enter**. If the date is correct, press **Enter**. If the date is incorrect, type the correct date, and press **Enter**.

5 Type **ver** and press **Enter**.

6 Type **cls** and press **Enter**.

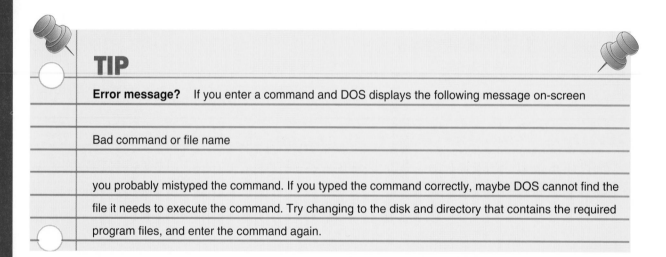

```
A:\>c: ——— Changes to drive C.

C:\>prompt $p$g ———

C:\>cd\dos ——— Changes to the DOS directory.

C:\DOS>date ——— Displays the current date.
Current date is Thu 05-13-1993
Enter new date (mm-dd-yy): 05-14-1993

C:\DOS>ver ——— Displays the DOS version number.

MS-DOS Version 6.00

C:\DOS>cls ——— Clears the screen.
```

Controls the appearance of the DOS prompt ($p tells DOS to display the name of the current directory).

TIP

Error message? If you enter a command and DOS displays the following message on-screen

Bad command or file name

you probably mistyped the command. If you typed the command correctly, maybe DOS cannot find the file it needs to execute the command. Try changing to the disk and directory that contains the required program files, and enter the command again.

CHANGING TO A DISK DRIVE

Why Change Disk Drives?

To run a program or work with the files on a disk, you must tell DOS which disk drive to activate. DOS will then look to the current disk drive whenever you specify one or more files with which to work.

Remember, most computers have at least three disk drives, designated as A, B, and C. The floppy drives are A and B, and the hard disk drive (usually inside the computer) is C.

Changing Disk Drives

1 Make sure there is a disk in the drive to which you want to change. (If the disk is blank, it must be formatted. If the disk has files on it, it is already formatted. If you are switching to a hard disk drive, the disk is permanently sealed inside the drive.)

2 Type the letter of the drive followed by a colon.

3 Press **Enter**.

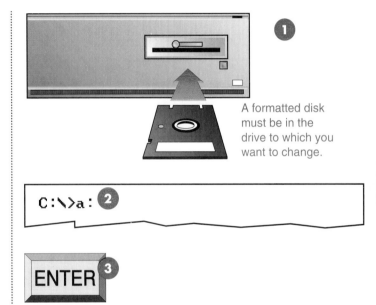

A formatted disk must be in the drive to which you want to change.

`C:\>a:`

ENTER

TIP

Error message?   If you forgot to insert a disk in the drive, the following message appears on-screen:

```
Not ready reading drive A
Abort, Retry, Fail?
```

If you inserted an unformatted disk, the following message appears on-screen:

```
General Failure reading drive B
Abort, Retry, Fail?
```

In either case, insert a formatted disk in the drive and press **R** for Retry and then change to a drive that

has a formatted disk in it. Or, press F for Fail, type C: and press Enter.

Working with DOS and Windows

CHANGING TO A DIRECTORY

Why Change Directories?

Before you can work with the files in a given directory, you must change to (activate) that directory. To change to a directory in DOS, you use the **CHDIR** or **CD** command, both of which stand for Change Directory.

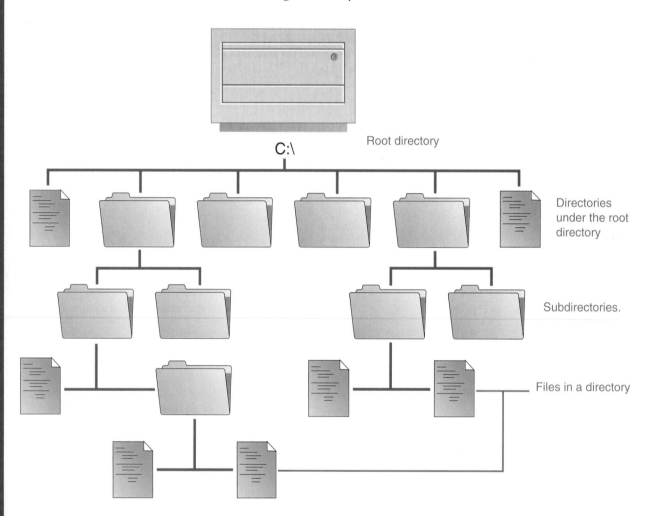

C:\   Root directory

Directories under the root directory

Subdirectories.

Files in a directory

LEARNING THE LINGO

Directory: A logical division of a disk that is used to store a group of related files. You create directories on a disk in order to keep files organized.

Ways to Change Directories

1 To change to the root directory (the first directory on the disk), type **cd**.

```
C:\DATA\SHOWME>cd\
```
1

2 Press **Enter**.

ENTER **2**

3 To change to a subdirectory of the root directory (a directory just under the root directory), type **cd\ *dirname*** where *dirname* is the name of the directory to which you want to change.

```
C:\>cd\data
```
3

4 Press **Enter**.

ENTER **4**

5 To change to a subdirectory of the current directory, type **cd *subdir*** where *subdir* is the name of the subdirectory to which you want to change.

```
C:\DATA>cd showme
```
5

6 Press **Enter**.

ENTER **6**

7 To change to a specific subdirectory, type **cd** followed by a complete path to the subdirectory.

```
C:\DATA\SHOWME>cd\windows\system
```
7

8 Press **Enter**.

ENTER **8**

Working with DOS and Windows

MAKING AND DELETING DIRECTORIES

Why Use Separate Directories?

A hard disk may contain hundreds or thousands of files. To keep the files from getting mixed up and lost, you should group the files in separate directories for better organization.

To make a directory, you use the **DOS MKDIR** or **MD** (Make Directory) command followed by the name you want to give to the directory.

To remove an empty directory at the DOS prompt, you must use the **RMDIR** or **RD** command, both of which stand for Remove Directory.

Making a Directory

1 Type **d:** where *d* is the letter of the drive on which you want to create the new directory.

2 Press **Enter**.

3 Type **cd ***dirname* where *dirname* is the directory where you want the new directory to appear.

4 Press **Enter**.

5 Type **md *dirname***, where *dirname* is the name for the new directory.

```
D:\DATA>md letters
```
5

6 Press **Enter**.

6

7 To change to the new directory, type **cd *dirname***, where *dirname* is the name of the new directory.

```
D:\DATA>cd letters
```
7

8 Press **Enter**.

ENTER **8**

```
D:\DATA\LETTERS>
```
New directory is a subdirectory of \DATA.

TIP

Directory name rules A directory name can consist of up to eight characters with a three character extension (just like a file name). You can use any characters except the following:

$$ " \ . \ / \ \backslash \ [\ ] \ : \ * \ < \ > \ | \ + \ ; \ , \ ? $$

Omit the extension; it is difficult to work with.

Working with DOS and Windows

MAKING AND DELETING DIRECTORIES

Deleting an Empty Directory

1 Type **cd ***dirname* where *dirname* is the directory just above the directory you want to remove.

```
D:\DATA\LETTERS>cd\data
```

2 Press **Enter**.

ENTER

3 Type **rd** *dirname*, where *dirname* is the name of the directory you want to remove.

```
D:\DATA>rd letters
```

4 Press **Enter**. DOS removes the directory.

ENTER

```
D:\DATA>cd letters
Invalid directory
```

If you try to change to the deleted directory, DOS tells you that the directory does not exist.

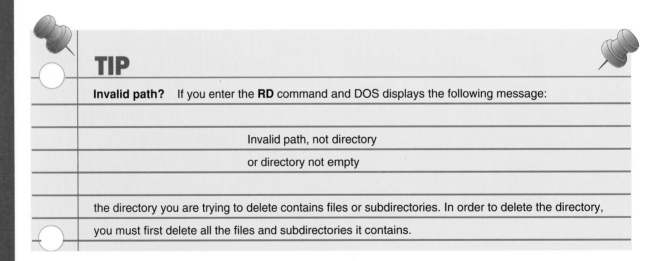

TIP

Invalid path? If you enter the **RD** command and DOS displays the following message:

Invalid path, not directory

or directory not empty

the directory you are trying to delete contains files or subdirectories. In order to delete the directory, you must first delete all the files and subdirectories it contains.

DISPLAYING A LIST OF FILES

Why View a List of Files?

Many times, you may be unsure whether a particular file is in a given directory, or you may be unsure of the file's exact name. When this happens, you can view the names of the files in the current directory.

Viewing a File List

1 Type **d**: where *d* is the letter of the drive that contains the list of files you want to view.

2 Press **Enter**.

3 Type **cd \dirname** where *dirname* is the directory that contains the list of files you want to view.

4 Press **Enter**.

Working with DOS and Windows

DISPLAYING A LIST OF FILES

5 Type **dir**.

```
C:\DOS>dir 5
```

6 Press **Enter**.

ENTER **6**

TIP

List too long?   If the file list contains too many files to fit on one screen, the list scrolls off the top of

the screen. To prevent the list from scrolling off the screen, you have two options:

1. Type **dir /w** (**w** stands for

   Wide), and press **Enter**.

2. Type **dir /p** (**p** stands

   for Pause), and press **Enter**.

   Press any key to see the next

   screenful of names.

```
Volume in drive C is JOE KRAYNAK
Volume Serial Number is 1A54-6AA9
Directory of C:\DOS

[.]            [..]           DBLSPACE.BIN   FORMAT.COM     FORMAT!.COM
NLSFUNC.EXE    COUNTRY.SYS    KEYB.COM       KEYBOARD.SYS   ANSI.SYS
ATTRIB.EXE     CHKDSK.EXE     EDIT.COM       EXPAND.EXE     MORE.COM
MSD.EXE        EDLIN.EXE      QBASIC.EXE     RESTORE.EXE    SYS.COM
UNFORMAT.COM   MIRROR.COM     NETWORKS.TXT   README.TXT     SMARTDRV.SYS
UNDELET!.EXE   DEBUG.EXE      FDISK.EXE      DOSSHELL.VID   MEMMAKER.STS
DOSSHELL.GRB   CHOICE.COM     DEFRAG.EXE     DEFRAG.HLP     MSBACKUP.LOG
DEFAULT.SET    DOSSWAP.EXE    PACKING.LST    EGA.CPI        APPNOTES.TXT
EGA.SYS        HIMEM.SYS      RECOVER.EXE    DOSSHELL.EXE   MEM.EXE
XCOPY.EXE      DELTREE.EXE    MONEY.BAS      MSHERC.COM     MOVE.EXE
GORILLA.BAS    4201.CPI       4208.CPI       5202.CPI       RAMDRIVE.SYS
ASSIGN.COM     SMARTDRV.EXE   DISPLAY.SYS    DOSHELP.HLP    COMP.EXE
DOSSHELL.COM   FASTHELP.EXE   DOSHELP.EXE    EDIT.HLP       FASTOPEN.EXE
GRAFTABL.COM   HELP.HLP       HELP.COM       MODE.COM       POWER.EXE
NIBBLES.BAS    REMLINE.BAS    PRINT.EXE      QBASIC.HLP     EXE2BIN.EXE
SHARE.EXE      JOIN.EXE       LCD.CPI        SETVER.EXE     PRINTER.SYS
APPEND.EXE     DELOLDOS.EXE   DISKCOMP.COM   DOSHELP.CP8    DISKCOPY.COM
DEFAULT.BAK    DRIVER.SYS     DEFAULT.SLT    PAM.CIF        SHELL.CLR
FC.EXE         FIND.EXE       GRAPHICS.COM   KEYB40.COM     MODE40.COM
Press any key to continue . . .
```

The dir /w /p command displays
a wide list and pauses the list.

Exercise

Many times, you may not want to view all the files in a directory. You may, for example, want to view only those files that have the **.EXE** extension or the **.COM** extension. To view a group of files, you can use *wild-card characters*. Type the following commands to practice using wild-card characters:

1 Type **c:** and press **Enter** to change to drive C.

2 Type **cd\dos** and press **Enter** to change to the **DOS** directory.

3 Type **dir *.com /w** and press **Enter** to display all the files with the extension .COM in a wide display.

4 Type **dir ???.*** and press **Enter** to display all the file names that have three or fewer characters.

5 Type **dir s???.*** and press **Enter** to display all the file names that start with s and have four or fewer characters.

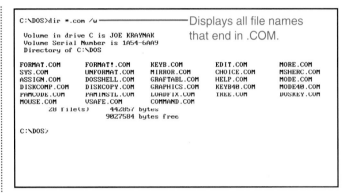
Displays all file names that end in .COM.

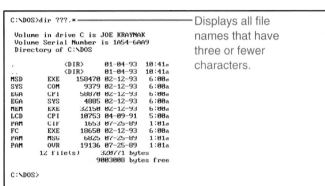
Displays all file names that have three or fewer characters.

Displays all file names that start with s and have four or fewer characters.

LEARNING THE LINGO

Wild-card character: Any character that takes the place of another character or a group of characters. The question mark (**?**) stands in for a single character. The asterisk (*****) stands in for a group of characters.

Working with DOS and Windows

FORMATTING A FLOPPY DISK

Why Format Floppy Disks?

If you get a box of new, unformatted disks, you must format the disks before you can use them to store files. You will normally format a disk only once (when it is brand new). If you format a disk that already contains files, the files are destroyed.

Before you start formatting disks, ask yourself the following questions:

What kind of floppy disk drive do I have? Is it high-density (1.2M or 1.44M) or double-density (360K or 720K)? Check the computer documentation.

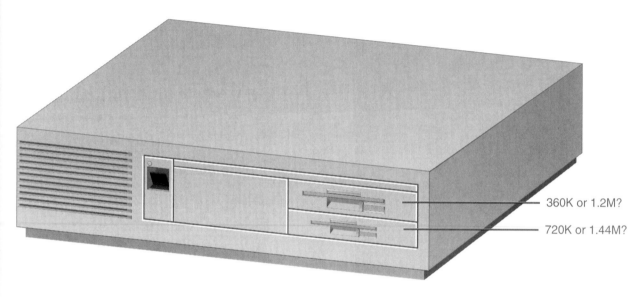

360K or 1.2M?

720K or 1.44M?

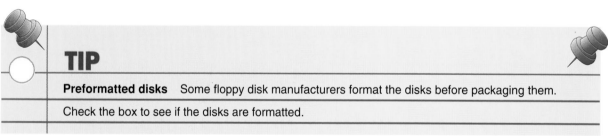

TIP

Preformatted disks   Some floppy disk manufacturers format the disks before packaging them.

Check the box to see if the disks are formatted.

What kind of floppy disks do I want to format? Do you have high-density or double-density disks? Check the disks or the box in which the disks came.

You cannot format a high-density disk in a double-density disk drive. For example, you cannot format a 1.2M disk in a 360K drive.

You can format a double-density disk in a high-density drive if you tell DOS specifically to do that. For example, you can format a 360K disk in a 1.2M disk drive.

Formatting a Disk in a Drive of the Same Capacity

1 Insert the blank disk into the floppy disk drive, and close the drive door, if it has one.

FORMATTING A FLOPPY DISK

2 Type **format** followed by a space, the letter of the drive that contains the blank floppy disk, and : (a colon).

```
C:\DOS>format a:
```

3 Press **Enter**. DOS displays a message telling you to insert a disk (which you have already done).

```
C:\DOS>format a:
Insert new diskette for drive A:
and press ENTER when ready...
```

4 Press **Enter**. DOS starts to format the disk.

5 When DOS is done formatting, it displays a message asking if you want to type a volume label. To label the disk, type a volume label (up to 11 characters).

```
C:\DOS>format a:
Insert new diskette for drive A:
and press ENTER when ready...

Checking existing disk format.
Saving UNFORMAT information.
Verifying 1.2M
Format complete.

Volume label (11 characters, ENTER for none)? Letters
```

6 Press **Enter**.

7 Remove the formatted disk from the drive, and store it in a safe location.

8 To format another disk, insert it into the floppy disk drive, and type **Y**. Otherwise, press **N** to stop formatting.

```
C:\DOS>format a:
Insert new diskette for drive A:
and press ENTER when ready...

Checking existing disk format.
Saving UNFORMAT information.
Verifying 1.2M
Format complete.

Volume label (11 characters, ENTER for none)? Letters

    1213952 bytes total disk space
    1213952 bytes available on disk

        512 bytes in each allocation unit.
    2371 allocation units available on disk.

Volume Serial Number is 322F-0FE9

Format another (Y/N)?n
```

TIP

Low-density disk in a high-density drive   To format a low-density disk in a high-density drive, you must add the **/F** switch to the **FORMAT** command to provide DOS with more detailed instructions:

- To format a 360K disk in a 1.2M drive, use the **/F:360** switch.

- To format a 720K disk in a 1.44M drive, use the **/F:720** switch.

Formats a 3.5-inch double-density disk in a high-density drive.

```
C:\DOS>format b: /f:720
Insert new diskette for drive B:
and press ENTER when ready...

Checking existing disk format.
Formatting 720K
Format complete.

Volume label (11 characters, ENTER for none)? Joe Kraynak

    730112 bytes total disk space
    730112 bytes available on disk

    1024 bytes in each allocation unit.
    713 allocation units available on disk.

Volume Serial Number is 0C1C-1000

Format another (Y/N)?n

C:\DOS>
```

TIP

Always specify a drive letter   Always follow the FORMAT command with the letter of the drive you want to use. With some versions of DOS, if you enter the FORMAT without specifying a drive letter, DOS will attempt to format drive C, your computer's hard drive. This would result in the loss of all of your programs and data on your hard drive.

Working with DOS and Windows

COPYING FILES

Why Copy Files?

You may want to copy a file from one disk to another to share the file with a friend or colleague, to transfer the file from a computer at home to one at work, or to create a duplicate file that you can change without changing the original.

Copying Files

1 Change to the drive and directory that contains the files you want to copy.

```
C:\DOS>cd\data①
```

2 Type **copy** *file1.ext d:\directory*, where *file1.ext* is the name of the file you want to copy, and *d:\directory* is the drive and directory where you want the file copied.

```
C:\DATA>copy mon7.txt b: ②
          1 file(s) copied
```

3 Press **Enter**. DOS copies the file.

TIP

Directory must exist   Before you can copy files to a directory, you must have created the directory. If you try to copy a file to a directory that does not exist, DOS will display an error message.

Copying Groups of Files Using Wild-Card Characters

Command	Description
copy *.doc a:	Copies all files that have the .DOC extension from the current directory to the disk in drive A.
copy chap09.doc b:	Copies only the file named CHAP09.DOC from the current directory to the disk in Drive B.
copy *.doc c:\samples	Copies all files that have the .DOC extension from the current directory to a directory named C:\SAMPLES.
copy *.* c:\samples\books	Copies all files from the current directory to C:\SAMPLES\BOOKS.
copy chap09.* c:\samples	Copies all files named CHAP09 (CHAP09.DOC, CHAP09.BAK, and so on) from the current directory to C:\SAMPLES.

Working with DOS and Windows

DELETING FILES

Why Delete Files?

If you are sure you no longer need a file, you can delete the file from a disk in order to prevent the disk from getting cluttered.

Deleting Files

1 Change to the drive and directory that contains the file you want to delete.

```
C:\DATA>b:  ❶
```

2 Type **del** *filename.ext*, where *filename.ext* is the name of the file you want to delete.

```
B:\>del mon7.txt  ❷

B:\>
```

3 Press **Enter**. DOS deletes the file.

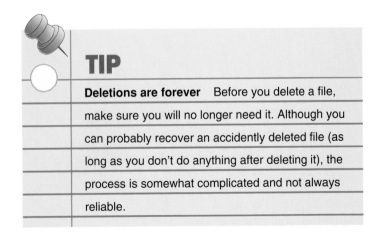

ENTER ❸

TIP

Wild card delete   You can delete a group of files by using wild-card characters. For example, to delete all files that have the **.BAK** extension, you would change to the drive and directory where those files are stored and enter **del *.bak**.

TIP

Deletions are forever   Before you delete a file, make sure you will no longer need it. Although you can probably recover an accidently deleted file (as long as you don't do anything after deleting it), the process is somewhat complicated and not always reliable.

USING THE DOS SHELL

Running the DOS Shell

If you have DOS version 4.0 or later (preferably version 5.0 or later), you have a program called the DOS Shell, which gives DOS a friendlier face. Instead of typing commands and file names at the DOS prompt, the Shell allows you to select commands from menus, change drives and directories by selecting them on-screen, and choose files from a list.

As you can see in the picture, the DOS Shell looks a lot different from the DOS prompt.

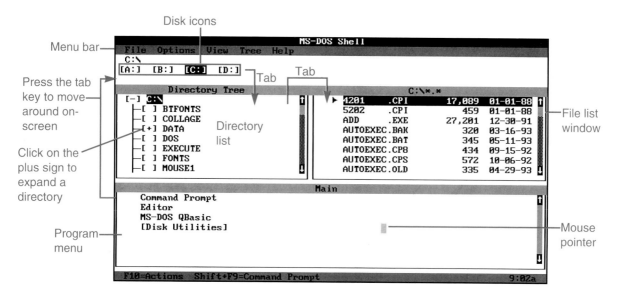

Disk icons

Menu bar

Press the tab key to move around on-screen

Click on the plus sign to expand a directory

Tab   Tab

Directory list

File list window

Mouse pointer

Program menu

Running the DOS Shell

Running the DOS Shell

1 Type **dosshell**.

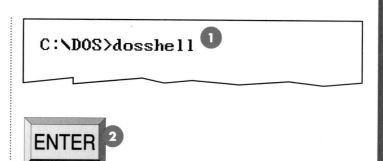

C:\DOS>dosshell ①

2 Press **Enter**.

ENTER ②

Working with DOS and Windows

Getting Around in the Shell

Menu bar   To open a menu, click on the menu name or hold down the **Alt** key while pressing the first letter in the name.

Tab   Press the tab key to move from one area of the screen to the other.

Disk icons   To change to a disk drive, click on its icon, or hold down the **Ctrl** key while typing the disk letter.

Directories   To change to a directory, click on it or tab to the directory tree, and use the arrow keys to highlight it.

Expanding a directory   To display the subdirectories of a directory, click on the plus sign (**+**) to the left of the directory name, or highlight the directory and type **+**.

File list window   To select a file, click on the file's name or use the arrow keys to highlight it.

Program menu   To run a program, double-click on the program's name or tab to the **Main** window, highlight the program, and press **Enter**.

TIP

Error message?   If the **Bad command or filename** message appears on-screen, take the following steps:

1. Type **c:** and press **Enter**.
2. Type **cd \dos** and press **Enter**.
3. Type **dosshell** and press **Enter**.

WORKING WITH DIALOG BOXES

Why Use Dialog Boxes?

As you work with the various DOS Shell commands, you will encounter *dialog boxes*. Dialog boxes are the Shell's way of asking for more information. You will type information into the dialog box or select desired items or settings from a list, and then enter a command to put your selections into effect.

Text boxes

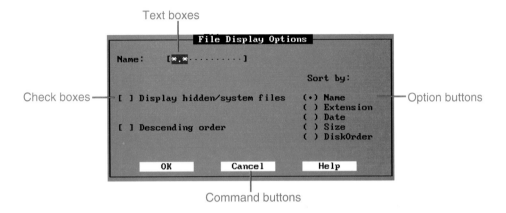

Check boxes —

Option buttons

Command buttons

List box —

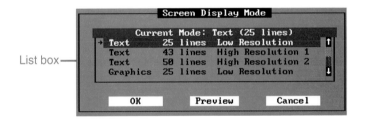

TIP

Moving around with the keyboard You can move from one area to another (one group of options to another) by pressing the Tab key. To move within a group of options, use the up or down arrow key. Use the Spacebar to turn a highlighted check box option on or off. Use the up or down arrow key to select an option button in a group of options. To select a command button, tab to it, and press Enter.

Working with DOS and Windows

Dialog Box Options

Name: [*.*· · · · · · · · · ·]

Text boxes allow you to type an entry. To activate a text box, click inside it or type the highlighted letter in the text box name. When you start typing, whatever you type replaces what is in the text box.

[ ] Descending order

Check boxes allow you to select one or more items in a group of options. To select an item, click on it or tab to it and press the space bar.

(•) Name

Option buttons are like check boxes, but you can select only one option button in a group. Selecting one button unselects any option that is already selected.

OK

Command buttons allow you to enter or cancel your selections. Once you have responded to the dialog box by entering your choices, you click on a command button or tab to it and press Enter to finalize the entry.

List boxes provide available choices. To select an item in the list, click on the item or use the arrow keys to highlight it.

```
         Current Mode: Text (25 lines)
→  Text       25 lines  Low Resolution      ↑
   Text       43 lines  High Resolution 1
   Text       50 lines  High Resolution 2
   Graphics   25 lines  Low Resolution      ↓
```

WORKING WITH MICROSOFT WINDOWS

What Is Microsoft Windows?

Microsoft Windows is a *graphical user interface* that runs on top of DOS and is designed to make your computer easier to use. With a graphical user interface, you don't have to type commands; instead, you select icons (small pictures that represent commands), and you choose commands from menus.

Control-menu box opens a menu which allows you to close the window or change its size and location.

Pull-down menu bar contains a list of the pull-down menus available.

Title bar displays the name of the window or program.

Minimize button shrinks the application window down to the size of an icon.

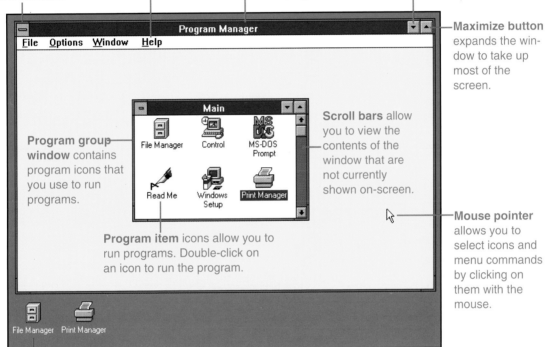

Maximize button expands the window to take up most of the screen.

Program group window contains program icons that you use to run programs.

Scroll bars allow you to view the contents of the window that are not currently shown on-screen.

Program item icons allow you to run programs. Double-click on an icon to run the program.

Mouse pointer allows you to select icons and menu commands by clicking on them with the mouse.

Application icons are shrunken program windows. You can restore the application to window status by double-clicking on its icon.

Starting Microsoft Windows

1 If necessary, change to the drive that contains your Windows files by typing the drive letter followed by a colon.

2 Press **Enter**.

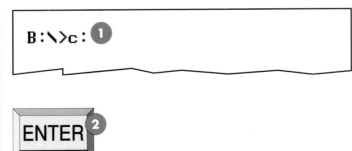

Working with DOS and Windows

3 Change to the directory that contains your Windows files by typing **cd \windows**.

```
C:\DATA>cd\windows  3
```

4 Press **Enter**.

5 Type **win** to start Windows.

```
C:\WINDOWS>win  5
```

6 Press Enter.

TIP

Quitting windows   To exit Windows, perform one of the following steps:

- Click on the **Control-menu** box in the upper left corner of the Program Manager window, and then click on **Close**.

- Double-click on the **Control-menu** box.

- Press **Alt+F4**, and then press **Enter**.

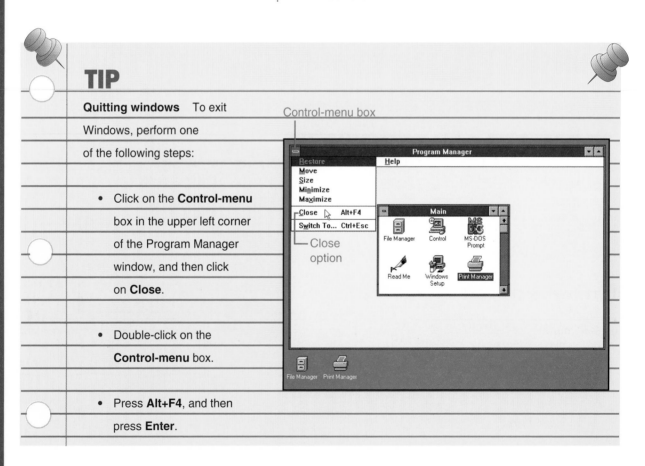

SELECTING COMMANDS FROM PULL-DOWN MENUS

Using Pull-Down Menus

Windows programs use pull-down menus to keep the commands out of the way until you need them. When you need a command, you simply pull the menu down and then select the desired command.

Open menu by clicking on the menu's name or by holding down the Alt key while typing the underlined letter in the menu's name.

Select a command by clicking on it or by typing the underlined letter in the command's name.

Menu bar conceals the menus until you need them.

Submenu appears if you select a command that is followed by a right arrow.

Ellipses follow any commands that open a dialog box.

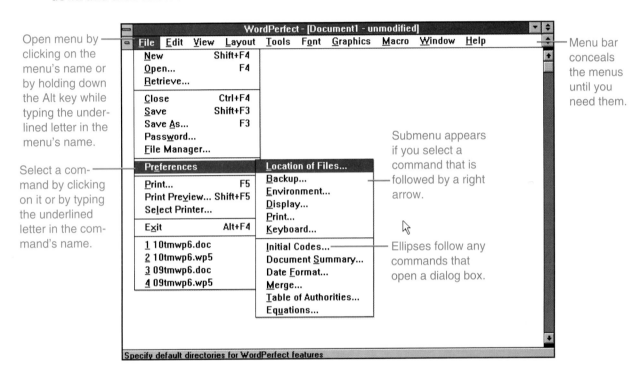

TIP

Quick menu change When a menu is open, you can open the menu to the left or right by pressing the left or right arrow key.

Working with DOS and Windows

RESPONDING TO DIALOG BOXES

What Is a Dialog Box?

Some commands on the pull-down menus are followed by an ellipsis (...). This shows that if you select the command, a dialog box will appear. Dialog boxes are Windows' way of asking for more information. You will type information into the dialog box or select desired items or settings from a list, and then enter a command to put your selections into effect.

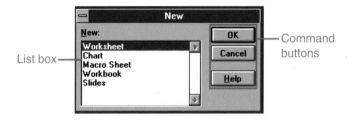

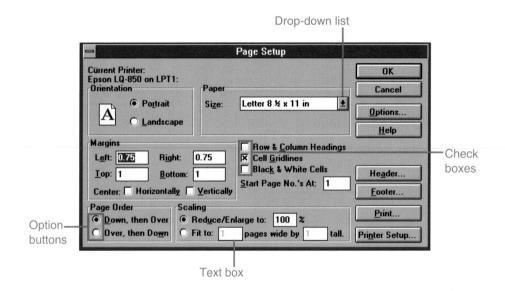

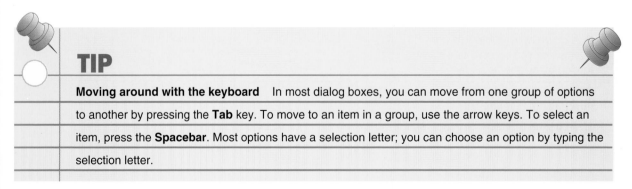

TIP

Moving around with the keyboard   In most dialog boxes, you can move from one group of options to another by pressing the **Tab** key. To move to an item in a group, use the arrow keys. To select an item, press the **Spacebar**. Most options have a selection letter; you can choose an option by typing the selection letter.

Dialog Box Options

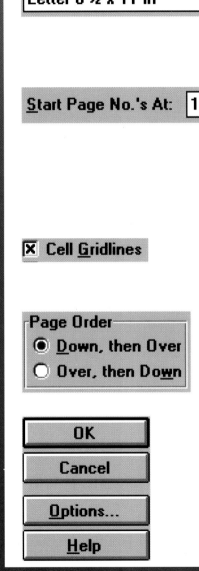

List boxes provide available choices. To select an item in the list, click on the item. If the entire list is not visible, use the *scroll bar* to view the items in the list.

Drop-down lists are similar to list boxes, but only one item in the list is shown. To see the rest of the items, click on the down arrow to the right of the list box.

Text boxes allow you to type an entry. To activate a text box, click inside it. To edit text that's already in the box, use the arrow keys to move the insertion point, the Del or Backspace keys to delete existing characters, and then type your correction.

Check boxes allow you to select one or more items in a group of options. To select an item, click on it.

Option buttons are like check boxes, but you can select only one option button in a group. Clicking on one button unselects any option that is already selected.

Command buttons allow you to enter or cancel your selections. Once you have responded to the dialog box by entering your choices, you click on a command button to finalize the entry.

Working with DOS and Windows

CONTROLLING WINDOWS

How Do You Manage Multiple Windows?

If you run two or more programs in Windows, the screen can get cluttered with multiple windows. You need some way to change from one window to another, resize windows, and arrange the Windows on-screen.

Moving a Window to the Top

If you can see any part of a window under a stack of other windows, the easiest way to move it to the top of the stack is to click on the exposed portion of the window. The window automatically jumps up front and covers anything under it.

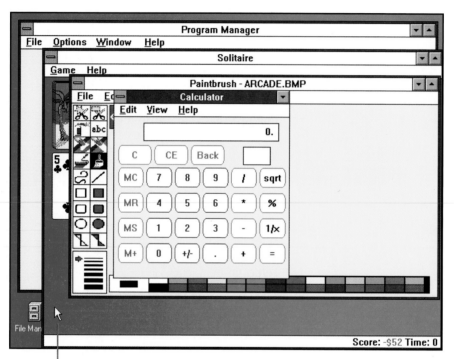

Click inside this window to move it to the top.

TIP

Completely covered? If you cannot see the desired window, Click on the **W**indow menu or press **ALT+W**, and then select the name of the window to which you want to go. The selected window is then moved to the front and is activated. If that doesn't work, press **Ctrl+Esc**, and then choose the window from the Task List.

Resizing a Window

As you are rearranging windows on-screen, you may want to resize the windows.

1 Move the mouse pointer to the edge or corner of the window until the pointer turns into a double-headed arrow.

2 Hold down the mouse button and drag the pointer toward the center of the window to make it smaller or away from the center to make it larger.

3 To maximize a window (so it takes up the full screen), click on the **Maximize** button.

4 To minimize a window (so it becomes an icon), click on the **Minimize** button.

5 To restore a window to its original size, click on the **Restore** button.

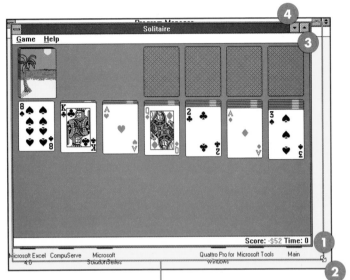

As you drag a border, an outline shows the new dimensions of the window.

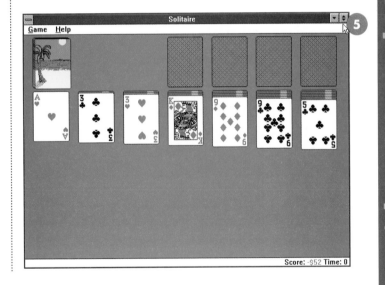

Working with DOS and Windows

Moving a Window

As you size and resize windows, you will probably want to move your windows around.

1 Move the mouse pointer into the window's title bar, and hold down the mouse button.

2 Drag the mouse pointer to move the window where you want it, and then release the mouse button.

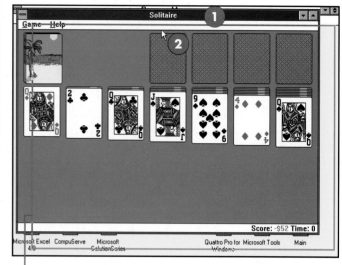

As you move a window, an outline shows the new location of the window.

TIP

Control menu In the upper left corner of every window is a Control-menu box that allows you to resize and move the window. To open the Control menu, click on the box or press **Alt+Spacebar** or **Alt+hyphen**.

PART 5

Making Your Computer Do Something Useful

The most important part of a computer is not all the components that make it up, but the applications (programs) that you can run on it. Application programs allow you to use your computer to do something useful, such as type a letter, calculate your taxes, and create business presentations. In this part, you will learn about the various applications you can run on a computer.

- Understanding Application Programs

- Typing with a Word Processing Program

- Crunching Numbers with a Spreadsheet

- Managing Your Data with a Database

- Painting, Drawing, and Creating Presentations

- Creating Your Own Publications

- Doing It All with Integrated Software

UNDERSTANDING APPLICATION PROGRAMS

What Are Application Programs?

An *application program* is a set of instructions that comes on disks and allows you to use your computer to perform a specific task.

Desktop publishing program: Lets you combine text and graphics to create illustrated pamphlets, newsletters, and books.

Word-processing program: Lets you type letters, contracts, memos, and books.

Graphics program: Allows you to draw or paint pictures.

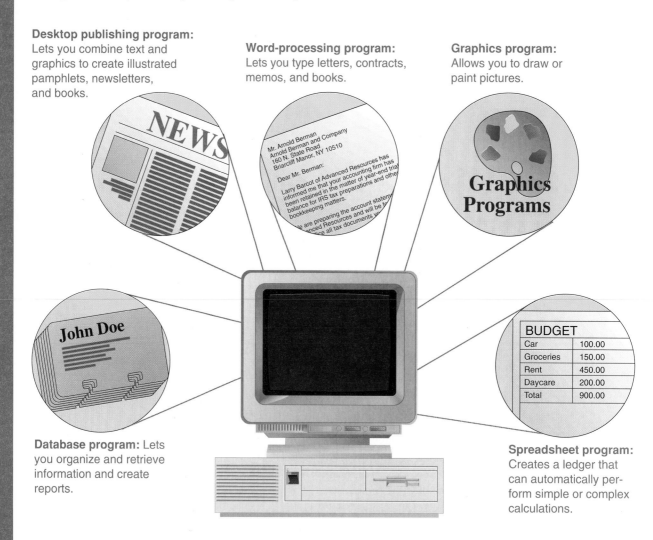

Database program: Lets you organize and retrieve information and create reports.

Spreadsheet program: Creates a ledger that can automatically perform simple or complex calculations.

TYPING WITH A WORD PROCESSING PROGRAM

What Is a Word-Processing Program?

A word-processing program allows you to type and print letters, reports, brochures, and other documents. Because a word-processing program treats the document electronically, it allows you to quickly and easily cut, paste, and move text around in a document. You can also save the document you create to a disk and then retrieve it later to edit it and fix your typos. Some sample documents you can create with a word-processing program are shown here.

RE: American Booksellers Association
DATE: June 3, 1993

What's Hot: Dinosaurs, comic books, fancy covers (embossing, matte, foil, etc.). Lukewarm: Voyager, interactive books.

The PHCP Editorial Board meeting will meet this Thursday, June 10, at 3:00 p.m. in the Board Room. The topic for discussion will focus on the titles that can be added to this fiscal year.

Memos and letters

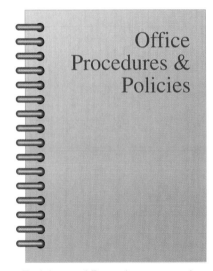

Office Procedures & Policies

Training and Procedures manuals

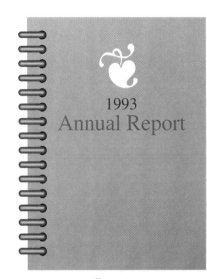

1993 Annual Report

Reports

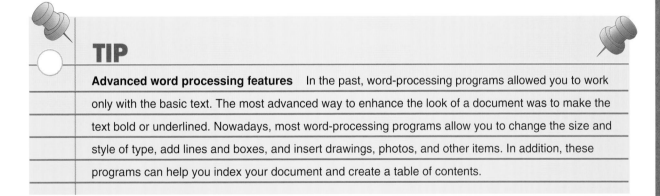

TIP

Advanced word processing features   In the past, word-processing programs allowed you to work only with the basic text. The most advanced way to enhance the look of a document was to make the text bold or underlined. Nowadays, most word-processing programs allow you to change the size and style of type, add lines and boxes, and insert drawings, photos, and other items. In addition, these programs can help you index your document and create a table of contents.

Making Your Computer Do Something Useful

TYPING WITH A WORD PROCESSING PROGRAM

Entering Text

To create a document, you first type the text.

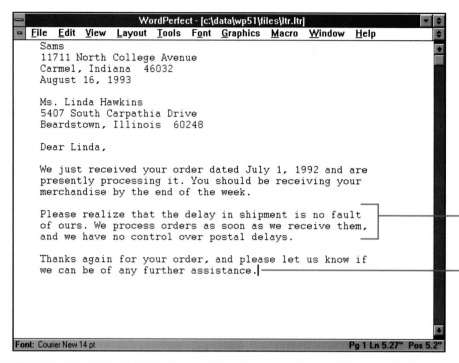

Word wrap The program automatically wraps text from one line to the next. Press Enter only to end a paragraph or short line.

Cursor or insertion point As you type, characters are inserted at the cursor or insertion point.

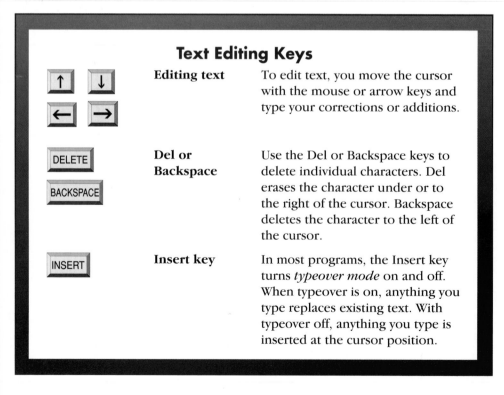

Text Editing Keys

Editing text To edit text, you move the cursor with the mouse or arrow keys and type your corrections or additions.

Del or Backspace Use the Del or Backspace keys to delete individual characters. Del erases the character under or to the right of the cursor. Backspace deletes the character to the left of the cursor.

Insert key In most programs, the Insert key turns *typeover mode* on and off. When typeover is on, anything you type replaces existing text. With typeover off, anything you type is inserted at the cursor position.

Whenever you start a program, certain settings (such as Typeover mode being on) are already in effect. These settings are called *defaults*.

LEARNING THE LINGO

Default settings: Settings that are in effect when you start a program. For example, most word processing programs assume you want to type in *insert mode*.

Working with Chunks of Text

Word processing programs allow you to cut and paste text in a document, so you can reorganize a document without retyping it.

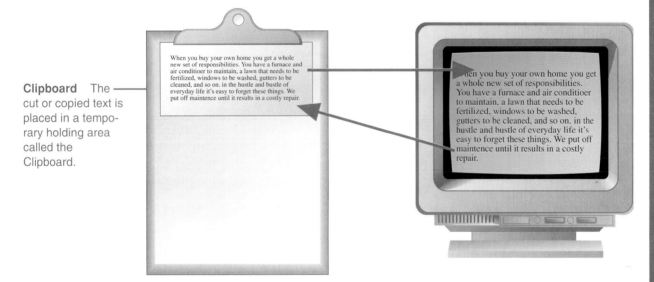

Clipboard The cut or copied text is placed in a temporary holding area called the Clipboard.

Cut or Copy You select text and then enter a command to cut or copy the text.

Paste After cutting or copying, you move the cursor where you want the text inserted and then enter the Paste command.

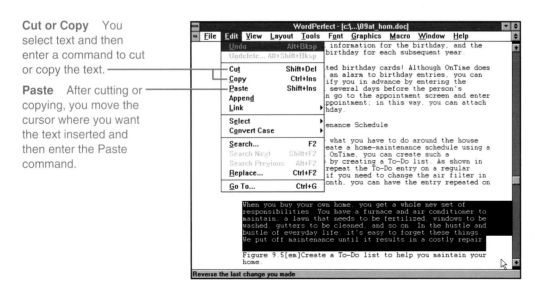

TYPING WITH A WORD PROCESSING PROGRAM

Formatting Your Document

With a word processing program, you have complete control over the appearance and layout of the text.

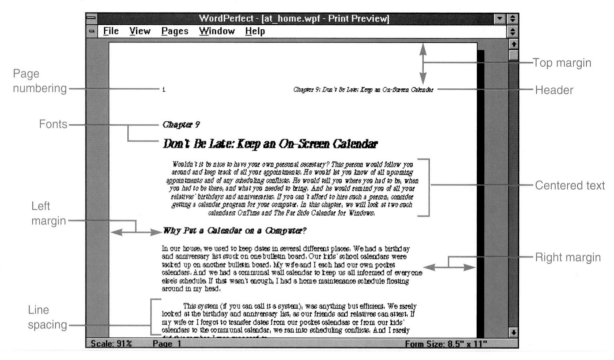

Formatting Options

Fonts
To emphasize key words and phrases, many word processing programs let you select from various fonts and type styles.

Margins
The margins tell the program how far to place the text in from the edges of the paper.

Page Numbering
Most word processing programs can automatically number the pages for you and print the page numbers where you want them.

Justification
You can change the alignment of text in relation to the left and right margins.

Line Spacing
You can choose to single-space or double-space your document.

Headers and Footers
You can add headers and footers to a document. A header is printed at the top of each page. A footer appears at the bottom of each page.

LEARNING THE LINGO

Font: Any set of characters that have the same *typeface* (design) and *type size* (measured in points).

Points: A standard unit used to measure the height of text; there are 72 points in an inch.

Type style: Any variation that enhances the existing font (for example, boldface, italics, and underlining).

Checking Your Spelling and Grammar

Most word processing programs come with features that check your spelling and grammar.

The spell checker compares each word in your document against the words in the spell checker's dictionary. If a word in your document does not match a word in the dictionary, the spell checker stops and lets you know.

The grammar checker scans your document for common grammatical errors, including overuse of the passive voice, subject/verb disagreement, wordy sentences, overly long sentences, incomplete sentences, and more.

Misspelled word

Choose from the list of suggested corrections...

... or type your own correction

Spell Checker

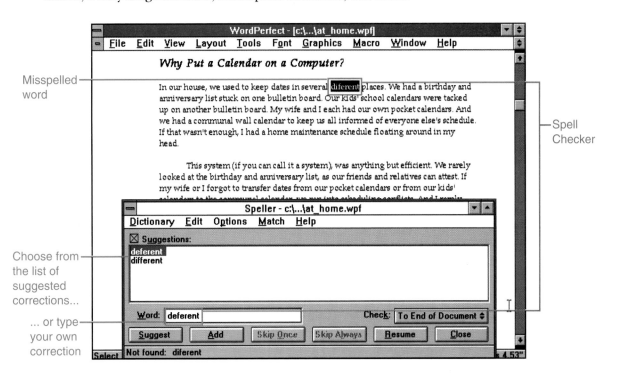

CRUNCHING NUMBERS WITH A SPREADSHEET

What Is a Spreadsheet?

A spreadsheet consists of a series of *columns* and *rows* that intersect to form small boxes called *cells*. Each cell can contain a label (text), a value (number), or a formula, which performs a calculation.

Because of their row and column format and their ability to perform complex mathematical equations, spreadsheets are commonly used to create balance sheets, income and expense statements, financial analysis worksheets, and payment schedules.

Cell addresses are used to keep track of the cells. The cell address consists of the column letter and row number. For example, the address of this cell is A2.

Columns run up and down the page and are usually represented by letters.

Rows run from left to right across the page and are usually numbered.

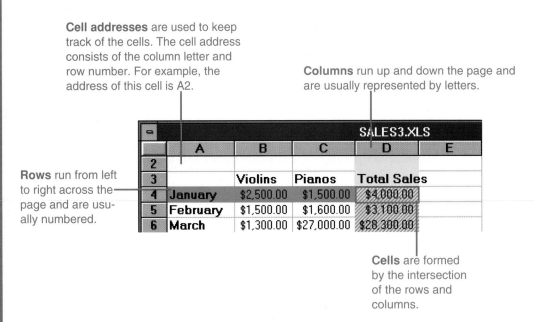

Cells are formed by the intersection of the rows and columns.

Creating a Spreadsheet

To create a spreadsheet, you type labels, values, and formulas into the cells.

Input line Whenever you move to a cell and start typing, your entry appears on the input line. When you press Enter, the entry is moved from the input line to the cell.

Status line Shows the address of the cell where the cursor is currently positioned.

Labels Text that describes the row or column.

Values Numerical entries.

Formulas Perform calculations on the numerical entries and insert the results.

Instant Calculations with Formulas

Spreadsheets use formulas to perform calculations on the data you enter. Formulas typically consist of one or more cell addresses and/or values and a mathematical operator.

This formula adds values in cells A1, B1, and C1 and divides the total by 3 to determine the average.

Mathematical operators indicate which mathematical operations to perform.

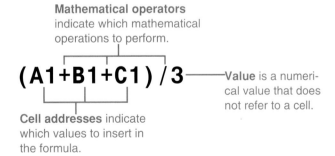

$$(A1+B1+C1)/3$$

Value is a numerical value that does not refer to a cell.

Cell addresses indicate which values to insert in the formula.

Making Your Computer Do Something Useful

CRUNCHING NUMBERS WITH A SPREADSHEET

Doing More with Functions

Functions are complex ready-made formulas that perform a series of operations on a specified *range* of values. For example, to determine the sum of a series of numbers in cells A1 through H1, you can enter the function @**SUM(A1:H1)**, instead of entering +**A1+B1+C1+** and so on.

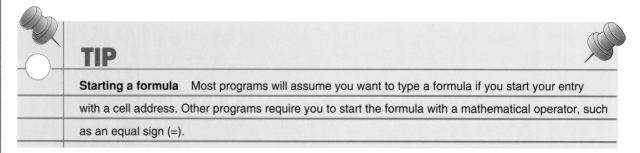

Function name (for example, SUM) indicates the operation that will be performed.

@ indicates that what follows is a function.

@SUM(A1:H1)

Argument (for example A1:H1) indicates the cell addresses of the values on which the function will act. The argument is often a range of cells, but it can be much more complex.

TIP

Starting a formula Most programs will assume you want to type a formula if you start your entry with a cell address. Other programs require you to start the formula with a mathematical operator, such as an equal sign (=).

Graphing Your Data

Newer spreadsheet programs can automatically graph the data in your spreadsheet.

1. You mark the cells that contain the data you want to graph.

2. Select a graph type.

3. The spreadsheet program graphs the data.

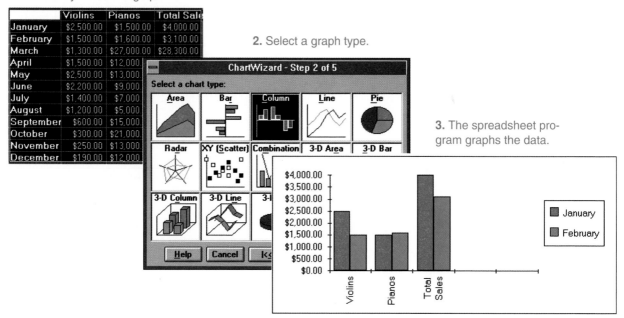

MANAGING YOUR DATA WITH A DATABASE

What Is a Database?

Databases are commonly used to store and manage information. For example, most libraries have a database that contains information about all the books in the library.

A database is a collection of *records*. Each record contains one or more *fields*, each of which contains one piece of data (a *field entry*).

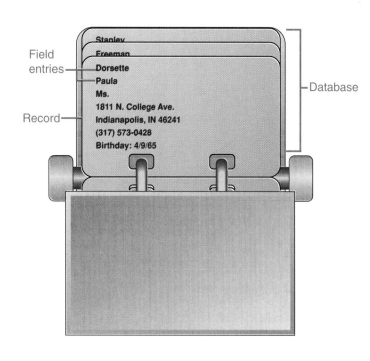

Field entries

Record

Stanley
Freeman
Dorsette
Paula
Ms.
1811 N. College Ave.
Indianapolis, IN 46241
(317) 573-0428
Birthday: 4/9/65

Database

Creating a Database

To create a database, you first create a blank form that contains the fields you will need in your database.

Use the form to create records. You type an entry in each field and then save the record. This dumps all the data into your database and displays a blank form so you can type information for another record.

Forms simulate, on the computer screen, the paper forms you fill out with a pen or pencil.

Field names show where to insert each piece of information.

ADDRESS2.WDB

Last name:
First name: Middle:
Title:
Address:
City: State: ZIP:
Phone:
Birthday:

MANAGING YOUR DATA WITH A DATABASE

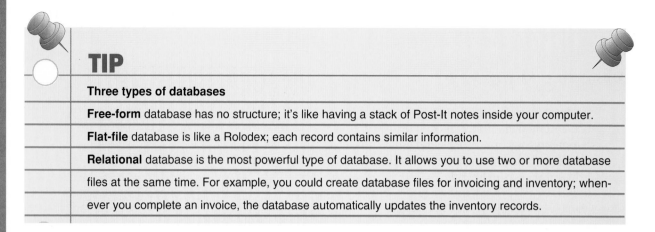

TIP

Three types of databases

Free-form database has no structure; it's like having a stack of Post-It notes inside your computer.

Flat-file database is like a Rolodex; each record contains similar information.

Relational database is the most powerful type of database. It allows you to use two or more database files at the same time. For example, you could create database files for invoicing and inventory; whenever you complete an invoice, the database automatically updates the inventory records.

Retrieving and Sorting Records

Once you have entered records into your database, you can sort the records in various ways and find specific records quickly. This is called *querying* the database.

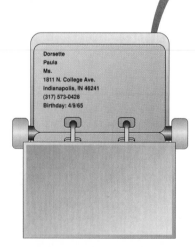

Search the database to view a selected range of records. For example, you can find records for people whose last name begins with D or whose ZIP code is 46032.

Sort records by specifying which field you want to use for the sort, whether you want the records sorted alphabetically or numerically, in ascending (A,B,C...) or descending (Z,Y,X...) order.

LEARNING THE LINGO

Query: The process of asking the database program to retrieve one or more records and/or sort the records.

Form: The computerized version of a paper form that you might fill out with a pen or pencil. Forms are used in databases to collect information.

Field: In a database, you enter each piece of data into a field.

Record: A collection of related data in a database. Think of a record as a completed medical form.

PAINTING, DRAWING, AND CREATING PRESENTATIONS

What Are Graphics Programs?

Computers are excellent tools for creating graphic images: paintings, drawings, graphs, technical illustrations, floor plans, and so on. In order for your computer to draw, however, it needs a graphics program.

Business Presentation Graphics

Presentation graphics programs are based on the assumption that most businesses require only a few graphic elements (often called *charts*): graph charts, text charts, organizational charts, and flow charts. As you can see in this picture, creating a chart is easy.

1. Pick a chart to specify the type of graph or text layout you want to use for the chart.

2. Enter the information you want the program to chart. The program automatically creates the desired chart.

3. You can combine text and graphs.

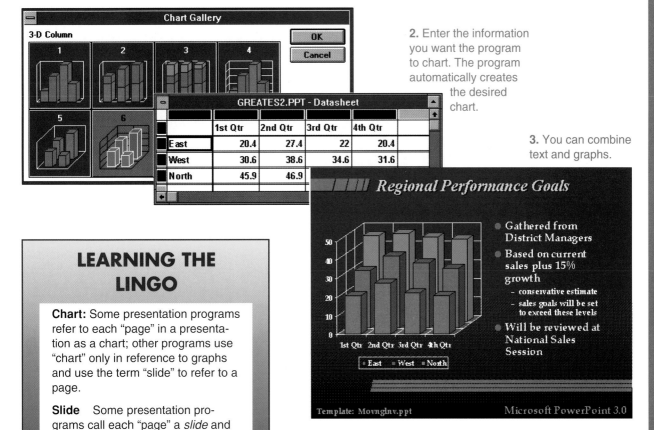

LEARNING THE LINGO

Chart: Some presentation programs refer to each "page" in a presentation as a chart; other programs use "chart" only in reference to graphs and use the term "slide" to refer to a page.

Slide Some presentation programs call each "page" a *slide* and refer to the presentation as a *slide show*.

PAINTING, DRAWING, AND CREATING PRESENTATIONS

Paint Programs

A paint program allows you to paint a picture on your screen. You can then use the picture in a presentation or paste it into a document using your word processing or desktop publishing program.

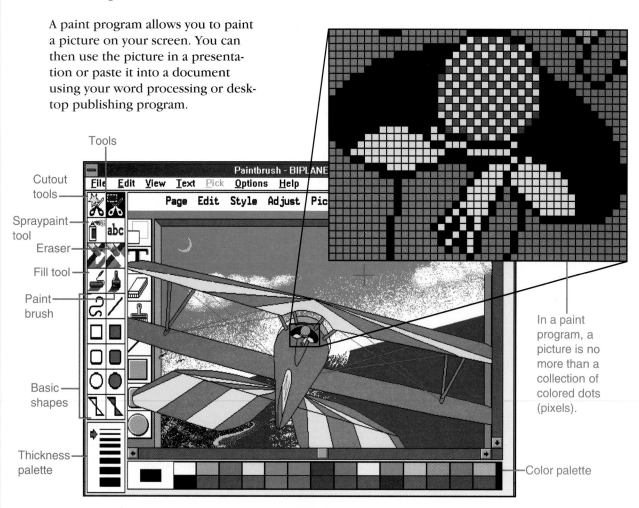

Tools

Cutout tools

Spraypaint tool

Eraser

Fill tool

Paint brush

Basic shapes

Thickness palette

In a paint program, a picture is no more than a collection of colored dots (pixels).

Color palette

📌

TIP

Transforming charts into slides

You can send files to a special service that converts the slides you create into actual 35mm slides.

📌

TIP

Professional help   Some presentation programs (PowerPoint, for instance) include *templates* (ready-made presentations) that were put together by professional artists. These templates specify a background color scheme for each chart, a place for a chart title, and other standard elements. You simply open the template and then change elements to customize it for your own use.

Parts of a Paint Program

Tools	A paint program comes with a set of tools that allow you to turn the on-screen dots (*pixels*) on and off and change their color.
Spraypaint tool	Acts like a can of spray paint. You hold down the mouse button and drag the tool across the screen to create a band of paint.
Paintbrush tool	Spreads "paint" evenly across the screen. When you drag the tool across the screen, you get a smooth, uniform ribbon of color.
Basic shapes	Consists of rectangles, circles, lines, and other shapes that you can place, move, enlarge, and stretch on-screen.
Fill tool	Allows you to fill a shape with color. You pick the color and then pour it into the shape.
Color palette	Lets you select the color you want to use for the various tools.
Thickness palette	Lets you select the width of the line created by the selected tool.
Eraser	Works like a chalkboard eraser. You drag it across the screen to remove any unwanted dots.
Cutout tool	Allows you to select a piece of the drawing in order to copy it or move it somewhere else.

LEARNING THE LINGO

Pixel: Also known as *picture element* or *pel*, a pixel is a tiny dot on the monitor. Any character you type or picture you draw consists of a pattern of pixels.

Object-oriented drawing programs: Drawing programs that treat an illustration as a collection of objects rather than as a collection of dots.

Vector graphics: A program that stores each object as a set of mathematical instructions that tell the program how to draw and print the object. For example, the instructions for a circle may tell the program where to locate the center of the circle and how wide to make the circle.

Making Your Computer Do Something Useful

PAINTING, DRAWING, AND CREATING PRESENTATIONS

Draw Programs

Unlike a paint program that treats a drawing as a collection of dots or pixels, a draw program treats a drawing as a collection of shapes: lines, circles, arcs, ovals, rectangles, and irregular shapes.

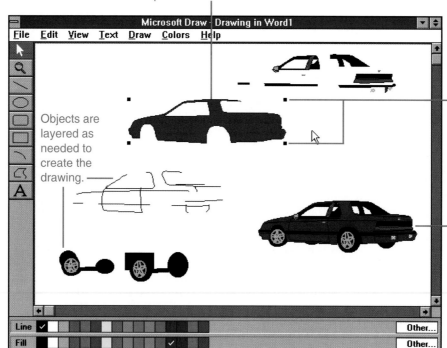

Fill objects with color or shading to produce the desired effects.

Objects are layered as needed to create the drawing.

Handles appear around an object when you select it. You can then copy, move, or delete the object by itself, without affecting surrounding objects.

Finished drawing

TIP

Ready-made art   An easy way to add graphics to a publication or presentation is to use clip art created by professional artists. Clip art consists of graphics files that are often included with word processing, desktop publishing, and business presentation programs. You can purchase separate collections of clip art on disk.

CREATING YOUR OWN PUBLICATIONS

What Is a Desktop Publishing Program?

Desktop publishing (DTP) programs are designed to work *with* word processing and graphics programs. The word processing program creates the text, the graphics program creates the graphics, and the desktop publishing program combines the text and graphics to create illustrated publications.

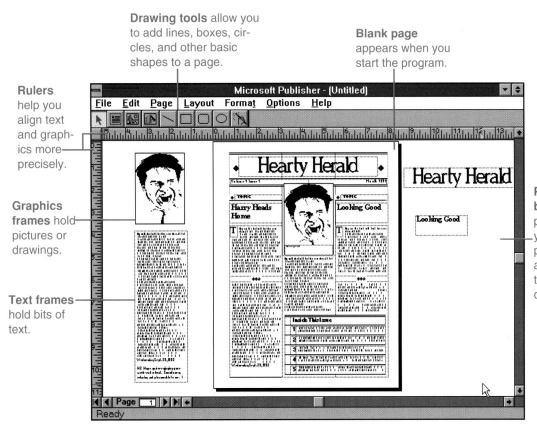

Drawing tools allow you to add lines, boxes, circles, and other basic shapes to a page.

Blank page appears when you start the program.

Rulers help you align text and graphics more precisely.

Graphics frames hold pictures or drawings.

Text frames hold bits of text.

Paste-up board around page allows you to drag pieces of text and graphics to the side during layout.

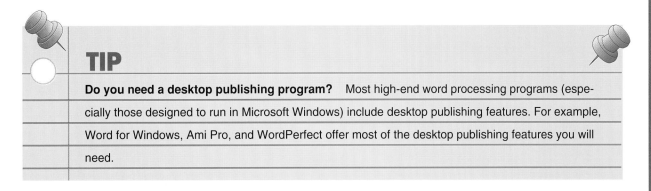

TIP

Do you need a desktop publishing program? Most high-end word processing programs (especially those designed to run in Microsoft Windows) include desktop publishing features. For example, Word for Windows, Ami Pro, and WordPerfect offer most of the desktop publishing features you will need.

Making Your Computer Do Something Useful

Working with Text

Most desktop publishing programs give you more control over the appearance of the text than you get in a standard word processing program.

Fonts allow you to control the size and style of the text. For example, you can increase the size of the headings and make them italic.

Borders around the text box can help give the text box a more graphic look.

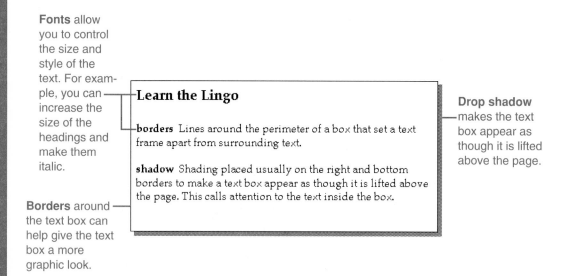

Learn the Lingo

borders Lines around the perimeter of a box that set a text frame apart from surrounding text.

shadow Shading placed usually on the right and bottom borders to make a text box appear as though it is lifted above the page. This calls attention to the text inside the box.

Drop shadow makes the text box appear as though it is lifted above the page.

Most desktop publishing programs offer a WYSIWYG (pronounced wizzy-wig) feature that shows you on-screen how each page will look in print.

LEARNING THE LINGO

WYSIWYG (pronounced "WIZZY-wig"): Stands for what-you-see-is-what-you-get. With WYSIWYG, the program displays a page as it will appear in print. Without WYSIWYG, text appears all the same size, and you may only see a box where the graphic object will appear.

Dragging Text and Graphics on a Page

With desktop publishing, you can manipulate the pieces of text and graphics on a page until the page looks just right.

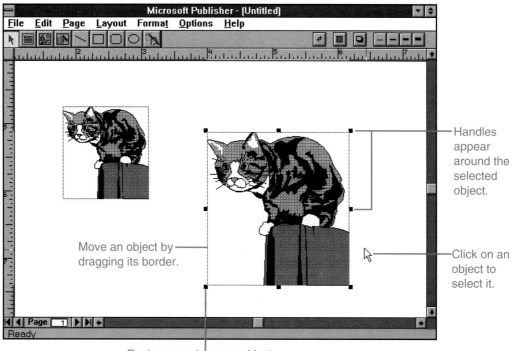

Handles appear around the selected object.

Click on an object to select it.

Move an object by dragging its border.

Resize or reshape an object by dragging its handle.

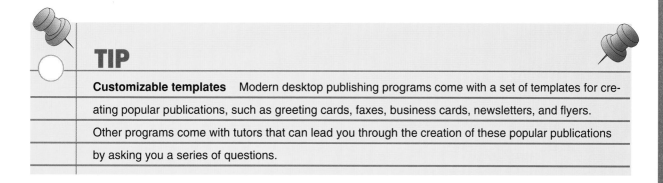

TIP

Customizable templates   Modern desktop publishing programs come with a set of templates for creating popular publications, such as greeting cards, faxes, business cards, newsletters, and flyers. Other programs come with tutors that can lead you through the creation of these popular publications by asking you a series of questions.

Making Your Computer Do Something Useful

DOING IT ALL WITH INTEGRATED SOFTWARE

What Is Integrated Software?

Integrated software is the Swiss army knife of software packages. In a single package, you usually get a word processing program, a spreadsheet and/or database program, a communications program (for your modem), and a graphics program (often for one low introductory price).

Microsoft Works for Windows includes a Word-Processor, Spreadsheet, and Database. You can access a drawing program from within the word processor.

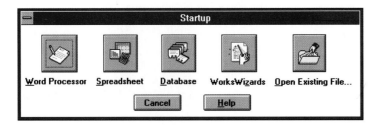

Integrated programs have three basic advantages:

They are easy to learn: All programs in the group have a consistent look and feel, making it easy to learn each program. For example, once you learn how to print a file in one program, you know how to print a file in all the other programs.

They work together: The file formats used in each program are *compatible,* so you can cut and paste data from one file into another. For example, you can cut a picture created in the graphics program and paste it into a letter created in the word-processing program.

They are cheap: You get several programs for the price of one.

However, going integrated may not be the best solution for all people. For instance, you may not need all the programs in the package, and the programs you get may not have the advanced features of a specialized program.

Glossary

access time   The average time it takes a drive to move its read/write head to a specified area on the disk.

application   A program that allows you to use your computer to do useful tasks, such as writing letters and keeping an address book.

backup   A copy of one or more files that are kept in case the original files ever get damaged.

BIOS   Pronounced "BUY-ose," stands for basic input-output system. The BIOS consists of startup instructions and other instructions that tell the computer how to manage input and output.

bit   The smallest unit of data with which a computer works. Because data is stored using a binary numbering system, a bit is either a zero (0) or a one (1).

bits per second   The number of bits that can be transferred per second (usually in reference to modems).

boot   To turn on your computer with the operating system instructions in place.

byte   A group of eight bits. Usually represents a character or a number from 0 to 9. For example, the byte 01000001 represents the letter A.

cache memory   Super-fast memory that is built into the central processing unit (CPU). ("Cache" is pronounced "cash.")

capacity   The amount of data that a disk can store. Capacity is typically measured in kilobytes and megabytes.

CD-ROM   Stands for Compact Disk Read-Only Memory. A storage system that uses laser technology to read data off compact disks. These disks often include text, graphics, short movie clips, music, and voices.

cell   In a spreadsheet, the box formed by the intersection of a column and row.

central processing unit (CPU)   The chip that processes all of the data that flows through the system unit.

CGA (Color Graphics Adapter)   A type of monitor that displays one color in 200 by 640 dpi (dots per inch) or four colors in 200 by 320 dpi.

check box   A box to the left of a dialog box option. When you select the option, an **X** appears inside the box, indicating that the option is active.

click   To point at something on-screen with the mouse and then press and release the mouse button.

clipboard   A temporary holding area for text or graphics.

107

GLOSSARY

CMOS   Pronounced "SEA-moss," CMOS stands for complementary metal-oxide semiconductor. CMOS is battery-operated memory that keeps track of how many disk drives your computer has, today's date and time, and other useful information about your computer.

columns   In a spreadsheet, the columns run up and down the page and are usually represented by letters.

command   An order that you tell the computer to carry out.

command buttons   In a dialog box, command buttons allow you to give your final okay or cancel the operation.

conventional memory   The 640 kilobytes of memory that comes with all IBM PCs and PC compatibles and is used for storing program instructions and data.

cursor   A blinking box or underline that shows where the text will appear when you type.

database program   A program that helps you store, manage, and analyze your data.

default settings   Settings that are in effect when you start a program.

delimiters   Spaces and special characters that break down a command line for DOS.

density   A measure of how much data can be crammed on a disk in a given amount of space.

desktop publishing program (DTP)   A program that lets you combine text and graphics to create illustrated pamphlets, newsletters, and books.

dialog box   A box that appears when you select a command that requires additional input from you. You enter information, settings, and preferences into the box and then choose a command button to activate your settings.

directories   Logical divisions on a disk (usually a hard disk) that help you manage groups of related files.

disk   A magnetic data storage medium that is used to store files.

disk cache   A portion of RAM that stands between RAM and the disk. A disk cache helps speed up the computer by cutting down on the number of times the computer must get information from the disk.

DOS   Short for Disk Operating System, DOS is the most common operating system in use today.

DOS shell   A program that makes DOS easier to use.

dot-matrix printer   A printer that creates characters and pictures as collections of tiny dots.

double-click   To enter a command or activate the item you are pointing to, by quickly pressing and releasing the mouse button twice.

drag   The process of holding down the mouse button while moving the mouse.

drive bay   An empty place in your computer that allows you to install a disk drive later. Think of it as a place in your car's dashboard where you can install a tape player.

EGA (Enhanced Graphics Adapter)   A type of monitor that can display 16 colors simultaneously in a resolution of 350 by 640 dpi. EGA monitors are obsolete.

expanded memory   Additional memory that swaps data into and out of conventional memory (640K RAM) at high speeds, giving the user the impression that the computer has more random-access memory (RAM) than the conventional 640K.

expansion slots   Sockets on the motherboard that allow you to connect additional circuit boards to the motherboard.

extended memory   Additional memory that acts just like conventional memory. Some computers come with additional memory, while others allow you to add memory later.

extension   Characters added to the end of a file name that usually represent the type of file.

field   In a database, you enter each piece of data into a field.

field name   A label used in a database program to show the user where to enter a piece of data.

file   A collection of related data. A *file* is like a folder that you might use to store a report or a letter.

file name   A label that you give a file so you can tell what is in the file.

flat-file database   A database program that allows you to work with one database file at a time.

floppy disk drive   A drive (usually on the front of the system unit) that can read or write to floppy disks.

font   Any set of characters that have the same *typeface* (design) and *type size* (measured in points).

formatting (disks)   The process of organizing the storage areas on disk so data can be stored in known locations.

formatting (documents)   The process of manipulating the appearance and layout (rather than the content) of the document.

forms   The computerized version of a paper form that you might fill out with a pen or pencil. Forms are used in databases to collect information.

GLOSSARY

formula   A mathematical sentence used in a spreadsheet program that tells the spreadsheet how to carry out an operation.

free-form database   A database program that has little or no structure; it's like having a stack of Post-It notes inside your computer.

full backup   A copy of all the files on your hard disk.

function   A complex, ready-made formula used in a spreadsheet program to perform calculations.

function keys   A set of F keys (F1 through F10 or F12) that are typically used to enter program commands quickly.

graphical user interface (GUI)   A program that is designed to make your computer easier to use. With a graphical user interface, you don't have to type commands; instead, you select icons (small pictures that represent commands), and you choose commands from menus.

graphics program   A program that allows you to draw or paint pictures.

hard disk drive   A disk drive (usually inside the system unit) that acts like a giant floppy disk drive complete with nonremovable disks.

incremental backup   A copy of only the files that have been changed or added since the last backup. These backed up files are added to the end of the full backup.

inkjet printer   A printer that creates characters and lines by spraying ink on the paper.

insertion point   Similar to the cursor, the insertion point is a vertical bar that shows where text will appear when you type.

keyboard   A typewriter-like device that allows you to type, enter commands, and move around on-screen.

kilobyte   A measure of data equivalent to 1,024 bytes. Memory and disk capacity are usually measured in kilobytes or megabytes.

label   In a spreadsheet program, text that you type in a cell, as opposed to numbers or values. When formatting a disk, "label" is used to refer to the process of naming the disk.

laser printers   A printer that works like a photocopy machine to produce high-quality printouts.

list boxes   In a dialog box, list boxes contain several items from which you can choose.

mathematical operator   A symbol used in a spreadsheet formula to indicate which mathematical operations to perform, such as addition (+), subtraction (–), and multiplication (*).

megabyte   A measure of data equivalent to 1,024 kilobytes. Memory and disk capacity are usually measured in kilobytes or megabytes.

110

MIDI interface MIDI (Musical Instrument Digital Interface) lets you connect a musical instrument or synthesizer to the sound board. You can then record, save, edit, and play back music and other sounds.

modem (MOdulator/DEModulator) Pronounced "mow-dem," device used along with a computer to transfer data over the phone lines.

monitor A TV-like device that allows you to see what's going on as you type and enter commands.

motherboard The main circuit board in a computer, the motherboard contains the "thinking" parts of the computer, including the memory and processing chips.

mouse A pointing device that allows you to select items on-screen by pointing and clicking rather than by typing commands.

MPC (Multimedia PC) A standard used for multimedia equipment and software used to ensure that the equipment and software will work together smoothly.

multimedia The combination of text, sound, video, graphics, and animation for use in presentations. Multimedia presentations are often stored and played back using CD-ROM disks.

operating system A set of basic instructions that control the overall operations of your computer, such as saving data to disk. The two most common operating systems are DOS and OS/2.

option buttons A circle to the left of a dialog box option. When you select the option, the circle appears filled in, indicating that the option is active.

parameters Specifications added to the end of a DOS command that indicate the objects on which you want DOS to act.

path The disk letter and directory names that lead to the directory in which a file or group of files is stored.

pixel Also known as *picture element* or *pel*, a pixel is a tiny dot on the monitor. Any character you type or picture you draw consists of a pattern of pixels.

platters A stack of disks that is hermetically sealed inside a hard disk drive.

point To slide the mouse on your desk until the tip of the mouse pointer is touching the desired item.

points A standard unit used to measure the height of text; there are 72 points in an inch.

ports Receptacles on the back of the system unit that allow you to plug other devices into the system unit, including a keyboard, mouse, monitor, and printer.

POST (power-on self test) A series of tests that your computer performs on itself whenever you turn on the power to the computer.

111

printer   A machine that transforms the data inside the system unit into a printed form that you can read and share with others.

processor   Another name for the central processing unit. See "central processing unit."

program   A set of instructions that comes on disk and tells your computer how to perform a task.

pull-down menu   A list of commands that you can pull down from the top of the screen.

query   The process of asking the database program to retrieve one or more records and/or sort the records.

RAM (random-access memory)   Electronic memory that stores program instructions and data while the CPU is using it.

Read-write heads   A device used inside a disk drive to read and write data from and to the disk.

record   A collection of related data in a database. Think of a record as a completed medical form.

relational database   A database program that allows you to combine data from two or more database files.

Reset button   A button on the system unit that clears the computer's memory if the computer ever refuses to respond to your commands.

resolution   The sharpness of an image. Resolution is usually measured in dots per inch (dpi). The more dots per inch, the clearer the image.

ROM (read-only memory)   A special type of memory that the manufacturer uses to store your computer's permanent startup instructions. Typically, you cannot change the instructions that are stored in ROM.

rows   In a spreadsheet program, rows run from left to right across the page and are usually numbered.

scanner   A device that converts text or graphics from paper into an electronic form that a computer can handle.

sectors   Divisions of a disk. Each file you save is stored on one or more sectors.

SIMM (single in-line memory module)   When you install memory, you usually plug a SIMM (single in-line memory module) into a memory slot on the motherboard. The SIMM contains one or more RAM chips.

slide   Some presentation programs call each "page" a *slide* and refer to the presentation as a *slide show*.

software   Instructions that come on disk and tell your computer what to do and how to do it.

sound board   An expansion board that plugs into a computer's motherboard and provides the computer with increased sound capabilities.

spreadsheet program   A program that lets you create computerized ledgers that will automatically perform mathematical calculations.

status line   An area, usually at the bottom of the screen, that shows your current position in a document and your options.

surge protector   A device that protects the electrical components inside your computer from sudden jumps in power.

switches   Optional text added to the end of a DOS command that tells DOS how to carry out the command.

syntax   The order in which you must type the elements that make up a command line.

system unit   The main part of a computer, the system unit contains all the components that allow the computer to store and process data internally.

telecommunications program   A set of instructions used with a modem that lets your computer communicate with another computer over the phone lines.

text boxes   In a dialog box, text boxes allow you to type a specific entry (such as a file name).

transfer rate   The measure of how much information the drive can transfer from the disk to your computer's memory in a second.

typestyle   Any variation that enhances the existing font (for example, boldface, italics, and underlining).

uninterruptible power supply (UPS)   A backup battery that continues to supply power to your computer when a power outage occurs. This allows you to save your data before turning off the computer.

upper memory   A portion of the memory that comes with every computer and is reserved for system use.

value   In a spreadsheet, a value is a numerical entry.

VGA (Video Graphics Array)   A type of monitor that displays 256 colors with a resolution of 640 by 480 dpi. Enhanced VGA offers higher resolution: 800 by 600 dpi. Super VGA offers the highest resolution: 1,024 by 768 dpi.

video adapter   A circuit board that plugs into an expansion slot on the motherboard. A monitor plugs into the video adapter.

virus   A computer program designed to vandalize your system.

113

GLOSSARY

warm boot   The process of restarting your computer without turning the power on and off. Rebooting is performed by pressing **Ctrl+Alt+Del**.

wild card character   Any character that takes the place of another character or a group of characters. The question mark (?) stands in for a single character. The asterisk (*) stands in for a group of characters.

Word processing program   A program that lets you type letters, contracts, memos, and books.

WYSIWYG (pronounced "WIZZY-wig")   Stands for what-you-see-is-what-you-get. With WYSIWYG, the program displays a page as it will appear in print. Without WYSIWYG, text appears all the same size, and you may only see a box where the graphic object will appear.

Index

Index